DESTINATION
IDAHO

Tim Woodward

ISBN: 0615535925
ISBN 13: 9780615535920

Editor: Niki Forbing-Orr
Cover design: Shawn Raecke
Cover photo: Darin Oswald

Other books by Tim Woodward

"Shirttail Journalist"
"McCracker Takes a Vacation"
"Here in Curmudgeons' Corner"
"Tiger on the Road; the Life of Vardis Fisher"
"Is Idaho in Iowa?"
"The Department of Yarns"
"Quintessential Boise: An Architectural Journey (with Charles Hummel)"

TABLE OF CONTENTS

FOREWORD

The title of this book is taken from an irregular series I wrote for roughly a third of my career, but its meaning goes deeper. Idaho, its people and their stories are mainly what I wrote about for all of my Statesman career. I've had a lifelong love affair with my home state. Its ever-changing beauty and endless supply of fascinating characters never stop amazing me.

The hardest part of putting this book together was deciding what — and what not — to put in it. When the Statesman archives went digital in 1992, the newsroom's then librarian handed me a banker's box with 20 years of my columns and stories in it. My first thought was, "This is it? Twenty years of my life fit in a lousy box?"

It moldered in an attic, all but forgotten, until I had to go through it, as well as the digital archives, to choose material for this book. Only then did I appreciate the magnitude of the job. It took weeks. There were stories I didn't even vaguely remember — tales totally erased from the memory banks. Those chosen represent less than one percent of my career output. If your favorite story or column isn't among them, my apologies. Many of mine aren't, either. With one exception — the final piece — none of the columns used in my previous column collections are repeated here. Readers who purchased those books shouldn't have to pay for re-runs.

A word about the home-remodeling and vacation-disaster columns. I wrote them more than 20 years ago and am still known for them. Altogether there were fewer than two dozen — out of a total of some 3,800 columns. The best were included in previous books, which is why they aren't in this one.

Unlike the other books, this one doesn't consist exclusively of columns. Though they were what resonated most with readers, columns comprised only about a third of my work during the last half of my career. Excluding the Destination Idaho stories and profiles wouldn't have felt right. Still, in deference to what readers said they loved, the majority of the space is devoted to columns. I could spend months on a proverbial "in-depth project" that elicited a collective yawn, and a column knocked out in less than a day would have readers commenting on it weeks later.

I'm a lucky man. My career spanned one of the golden ages of journalism — a time when newspapers were the primary purveyors of the day's big stories, advertising revenues bordered on the obscene and readers couldn't wait for their papers to hit the porch. Now newspapers are operating with skeleton crews and fighting for their lives.

I was fortunate to have been around when, at the drop of a story idea, I'd be on a train trip around the U.S. or a plane to the U.S.S.R, the U.K. or Albania. The job was almost never boring, which is part of why I stayed so long. Forty years passed like a long blink.

That wasn't the only way in which I was lucky. After 35 years of working for one newspaper chain, I worked for two more after the Statesman and subsequently its new owners were sold in less than six months. In my case, that meant that the best came last. My heartfelt thanks to the McClatchy Co., Mi-Ai Parrish, Vicki Gowler and Niki Forbing-Orr for showing me late in the game what people who worked at other papers meant when they said it felt like family.

And thanks to all of you.

Thanks for buying this book. Thanks to some of you for reading faithfully for four decades. Through the magic of written words, we became friends. That was just one of the many great things about my job. I became a journalist because I decided it was more important to do what you're good at and enjoy than it is to make a lot of money. It was one of the best decisions I ever made. Because of it, and because of all of you who read my work and shared your stories with me, I became one of the richest men in Idaho.

— *Tim Woodward, July 2011*

WOODWARD VS. THE WORLD

This Elvis isn't famous. He's insane. (Darin Oswald / Idaho Statesman)

Humor columnists fall victim to the most unlikely mishaps. We pitch our tents on red-ant hills, our dogs lock us out of our cars, we find an ocean of trouble in a thimbleful of paint. The world seems to conspire against us. Thus the title of this section.

The principle applies equally, though in a different way, to the serious columns in the section's second half. Though never a political writer per se, I did tend to rail against governmental absurdities and other outrages when it seemed justified. Occasionally it did some good, but mostly the people who could have made a difference ignored it. — Tim Woodward

Normal Clothes, Please
(June 25, 2007)

Expect to see me any day now in shorts with legs roomy enough to accommodate a small family.

On my feet will be shoes Bozo the Clown would have envied. My shirt will be striped or checkered; my hair will be spiked.

Beneath the shorts with legs the size of pup tents will be the ultimate indignity — a thong.

That's what we've come to in men's fashions.

Fashions always have been dictated by young people, of course, mainly teens and twenty-somethings. And that's fine. They're the ones who look best in clothes anyway.

But why should the rest of us have to wear what they do?

It hasn't quite reached the point that there's nothing but their clothes in stores. Most department stores, for example, still carry men's dress clothes. You'll find just what you need if you're trying out for, say, Skull and Bones or a seat on the stock exchange. Other types of traditional-looking men's clothes, however, are getting harder and harder to find. I don't think I'm exaggerating in saying that the situation is the worst it's been since the 1970s. (Nothing could actually be as bad as the '70s.)

For those lucky enough not to remember them, it was virtually impossible in the '70s to find any item of apparel other than socks and underwear that didn't look like it was pilfered from the set of "Disco Fever." My wife has a picture tucked away somewhere of me toddling around in platform shoes, checkered bell bottom pants and a shirt with puffy sleeves and a collar big enough to use as a dinner napkin. She gets it out and shows it to people on special occasions, mainly Halloween.

It wasn't that most of us wanted to go around looking like roadies for the Bee Gees; there wasn't a choice. Regular clothes were all but nonexistent. And it's hard not to think that we're heading down that road again.

Men's summer shorts, for example. The legs reach below the knees and are baggy enough to hide a watermelon. Elephants don't have legs that big. They're fine for teenagers, but for the rest of us they look ridiculous. Show me a sorrier fashion statement than a gray-haired geezer dressed like he's trying out for the Black Eyed Peas.

Normal jeans are losing the fashion battle to what I've come to call junk jeans. I've always gotten rid of my jeans when they ripped, but now they come pre-ripped, pre-ripped-and-stitched-back-together, pre-faded, even pre-stained. I went clothes shopping this spring and had to look for jeans that didn't look like they'd been soaked in crankcase oil. Not evenly, but soaked in a way that made it look like a mechanic had used them to wipe a shop floor. To my relief, the store had two pairs of "retro" jeans in my size — no rips, tears, faded spots, worn patches or stains. I bought them both, in much the way that you snap up rare and valuable items at a yard sale.

No such luck with shoes. The shoe department could have been a closet at Ringling Brothers. What law says that walking shoes need stripes, spots, holes, geometric patterns and gaudy colors? Why can't they just be shoes?

On the shelf where my favorite brand and style of underwear had always been was a display of thongs. Really, now, the percentage of American men who actually look good in thongs has to be miniscule. Brad Pitt in a thong is one thing; your Uncle Howard is another. For the life of me I can't imagine buying one, let alone wearing one.

Shirts? No problem — if you like checks or stripes.

It's absolutely true that fashions come back. Most of the casual shirts in stores today look exactly like the striped and checkered shirts my friends and I wore to grade school, which is why I can't bring myself to buy them. They may be the height of fashion, but to me they look hopelessly old-fashioned.

Fashion will always be for the young, but is it too much to ask that it throw a few crumbs to the rest of us? All I really want are some plain shirts in a nice fabric, some pants that don't look like they came off a rack at Jiffy Lube and a pair of comfortable, sensible-looking walking shoes. Is that too much to ask?

Maybe not. I actually found a few things like that a couple of weeks ago at a store in the outlet mall. They were on clearance, marked down to half price.

Maybe it's a coincidence, but the place was crawling with guys dressed just like I was.

Car Alarm Hell
(Sept. 10, 2008)

You know those annoying people who let their car alarms go off at eardrum-rupturing volumes and don't shut them off? I used to really hate those people — until I became one of them.

Before that, I had absolutely no patience with car-alarm junkies. Why couldn't they keep their stupid alarms from waking the dead? How hard could it be to just shut them off?

Actually a lot harder than you might think.

My car had an alarm installed by its previous owner when I bought it a little more than a year ago. I never paid any attention to it, because, mercifully, it never did anything.

That didn't seem to be a problem until I had it in the shop for something else last week and was told that it wasn't working because it was in something called valet mode. And in the unlikely event that it ever did go off in valet mode, the salesman said, it would be impossible to start the engine. That didn't sound like a lot of fun, so I had them take it out of valet mode.

It took about 15 minutes to realize that that was a serious mistake. That's how long it took to drive to a Downtown store where I needed to buy something. The store was closed so I decided to go home. At least that was the plan.

When the key turned in the car-door lock, it sounded like someone had released a swarm of chirping crickets. It was a new and somewhat startling experience; I'd never actually heard my car alarm before. For a novice, it was also a bit mystifying. Why would the alarm go off? You have to unlock your door to get in, don't you?

The chirping was just an introduction. Most car alarms are content with intermittent honking. Mine has an entire arsenal of sounds, all excruciatingly loud and each more obnoxious than the one before.

The chirping, which at least had been relatively quiet, gave way to a piercing noise that sounded like a yelping police siren. Then it was a series of unearthly shrieks, followed by something resembling the low-pitched honk of a fire-truck, only louder. There might have been gunfire and wild-animal sounds for all I know; it was so loud it all but liquefied my eardrums.

The setting for this was Main Street near the center of Downtown during the evening rush hour. The sidewalks were crowded with people. And every one of them was glaring at me as if I'd triggered the alarm on purpose and wouldn't shut it off, for the obvious reason that I was an annoying jerk who enjoyed this sort of thing.

Valet mode was suddenly looking pretty good.

The good news was that the guy at the shop had left a button dangling under the dash and told me to push and hold it if the alarm went off.

Unfortunately, that did absolutely nothing. No button has ever been pushed harder or held more fervently. It was pushed and held for something like 10 minutes, which seemed way longer than that. The crowd of bystanders, meanwhile, was getting ugly. People as far away as Meridian were wishing me dead.

Suddenly — don't ask me why — the racket subsided. Wanting nothing more than to make a quick and merciful getaway, I turned the key in the ignition.

The car wouldn't start.

Worse, the racket returned.

"Can't you see I'm trying to shut it off? I'm getting a blister from pushing this stupid button and haven't been this embarrassed in years, so quit staring daggers at me!"

That's what I wanted to say. Instead, I did my best to look pleasant and agreeable while praying that no one was carrying a concealed weapon.

That was when the guy came out of the music store.

"There are two guitar players in there giving lessons," he said.

Guitar players? How could they help? I play guitar myself and know for a fact that most guitar players are about as technologically proficient as field mice.

"That's not what I meant," he politely explained. "I meant that your car is making so much noise that they can't hear themselves giving lessons."

Great. Now my car alarm not only was disturbing the peace; it potentially was depriving the world of the next Jimi Hendrix. The man from the music store graciously offered to call the shop that had taken the alarm out of valet mode and ask what could be done to restore the peace. With directions over the cell phone, I was able to remove the alarm box and yank the wires loose.

The resulting silence was broken by a heartfelt cheer from a nearby bar. The alarm is disabled now.

Permanently.

If thieves want my car, they can have it.

This Is Not Slumbering
(June 26, 1988)

I'm writing this with my eyes closed.

There's a good reason for my eyes to be closed. They won't stay open.

My mouth, however, opens quite nicely. In fact, it's been open more or less continuously for the past six or seven hours.

My hair is a cowlick patch; my face is a stubble field.

My belt is crooked, my shoes are untied, my socks don't match. (A few things, in other words, have remained normal.)

On the way to work, I almost ran into a Subaru. The guy driving the Subaru was pretty upset. He rolled down his window and started shouting pleasantries like "four-eyed jerk" and "scum-sucking insect." I tried to tell him it was nothing personal; I almost ran into a Toyota before that, a curbing before that, and two doors and a wall before even leaving home.

The reason for my wilted condition was a party at my house. Not a normal party, with ashtrays and glasses overturned on the tables and adults overturned on the floors the next morning; it was far worse than that.

A kids' party.

Specifically, a kids' slumber party.

It was my daughter's birthday. She invited half the 12-year-old girls in the county. They came dressed in their cute little party clothes, carrying their cute little party presents, and dragging their cute little party sleeping bags along behind them.

It was a nightmare.

I knew it was going to be bad when, after watching videos, eating pizza, playing miniature golf, eating cake and ice cream and swimming until dark in a neighbor's pool, they ran in the front door shouting, "Now we can get down to some serious partying."

This was supposed to be the year I had them fooled. Experience has taught me that the best way for a father to survive a girls' slumber party is to isolate himself as completely as possible. So, I set up a cot and sleeping bag in the back yard, took a sleeping pill and settled down for a good night's rest.

The effect was the same as if Custer had worn a flak jacket to the Little Bighorn.

The problem was that the girls were playing a game that involved nonstop, high-decibel giggling, squealing, shrieking and screeching. The difficulty was compounded by 100-degree temperatures, meaning that the windows were open and the backyard "sanctuary" wasn't. A further complication was posed by the person designated to maintain order, my wife, who had locked herself in the bedroom and died.

And the mosquitoes. Don't forget the mosquitoes.

Around midnight, I braved the squeals and flying bodies (the game also involved gymnastics) long enough to come in for insect repellent.

Around 1 a.m., suffocated by insect repellent and 80-degree heat, I filled up the kiddy pool, slipped into my own birthday suit and had a long, cold soak.

Around 2 a.m., the neighborhood dogs joined the party.

Around 3 a.m., reeling from loss of blood (mosquitoes) and exhaustion (kids), I got up for another soak and another sleeping pill.

Or would have if I hadn't been locked out of the house.

There's something about a dripping-wet, naked man tapping on the window of a house filled with little girls at 3 in the morning that just isn't dignified.

It was about this time that the police car went by. I remained cool-headed, however, and calmly dove into a rose bush.

She wants to have another slumber party next year.

At the boarding school.

Instructions for Dummies
(Jan. 13, 1985)

Contrary to anything you may have read by Messrs. Buckley or Buchanan, the greatest threat to the national welfare is not communism.

Nor is it racism, sexism, fundamentalism or any other "ism."

The greatest threat to the national welfare, to say nothing of the individual welfare, is posed by the subversives who write the instructions that come with Christmas presents.

Logic would dictate that instruction manuals be logical and complete. Most are neither.

Take the instructions that accompanied a piece of computer equipment I bought a few days before Christmas. Having had experience with instructions, I made sure to ask if there were any inside the box, and if they were capable of being understood by a member of the English-speaking world. I was reassured on both points.

In fact, the box contained not one but two sets of instructions. The first, printed on a plastic bag, provided the sort of information every discerning computer operator needs to know:

"Do not put this bag over the head of a baby."

The second set of instructions, printed on a bag of silicon gel, were equally enlightening:

"Do not eat the silicon gel."

It seemed unlikely that anyone smart enough to run a computer would be blockheaded enough to eat a bag of silicon, but the instructions were quite clear. Also, they stimulated my curiosity. I began to wonder what silicon tasted like, which in turn made me hungry. So it wasn't really my fault that I put the plastic bag over the head of the nearest baby and bolted down the silicon gel.

This upset my wife. She said if she had known I was that hungry, she'd have warmed up the silicon gel in the microwave. With the cat.

The instructions typified those written for consumers at the lowest possible intelligence level. There really are people who try to dry their cats in microwave ovens. And I suppose there are even people obtuse enough to eat silicon gel, though it's hard to imagine any outside the Legislature.

The authors of such instructions couldn't care less if the customers get the products to work; they just don't want to be sued. This is why we have instructions warning us not to insert our feet in the blades of running lawn mowers, poke our fingers into the workings of operating television sets, or discipline our children by putting them in refrigerators.

Not many people are stupid enough to put their feet in running lawn mowers, their fingers into television sets or their kids inside refrigerators, but manufacturers cannot afford to ignore the legal threat posed by those who are. It's for them that the instructions are written, or rather for the luckless companies who are sued into oblivion for having such worthies as customers.

Many companies have adopted the practice of printing instructions that don't use writing, presumably because anyone stupid enough to do the things the instructions warn against wouldn't be able to read. That's why we have big red slashes through drawings of hair dryers in bathtubs.

How many people do you know who dry their hair in the bathtub?

Some instructions, in my opinion, represent an infringement of basic human rights. Signs in elevators, for example. Most elevators have signs saying what to do if the elevator stops. Invariably, the first words are: "Do Not Panic."

Think about that a minute. If you ask me, anyone who is in a stalled elevator and doesn't panic is a hopeless pervert.

Why shouldn't we panic? There aren't many situations left in which we can get away with panicking, and a stalled elevator is one of the best. If I want to panic in a stalled elevator, it's my God-given right and no one is going to take it away from me.

The opposite extreme of instruction-writing is exemplified by the manual that accompanied my Christmas gift to the family this year, a VCR. For those unfamiliar with the term, VCR stands for Very Complicated Recreation.

The first operating instruction said not to expose the VCR to rain or other moisture. This was mildly disappointing, as I'd been planning to use it in the bathtub while drying my hair.

Next came a set of 21 safety instructions, followed by directions for trial recording and playback. No mention was made of how to hook the VCR to the television set until Page 10, and Page 10 was written in Swahili.

It was Page 27 before there was an explanation of the basic operating controls. By then I had a headache from studying RF converters, 75-ohm coaxial cables and converter-descrambler boxes. In sign language.

The man at the store where I bought the VCR didn't seem to think there was a problem. He said all I had to do was follow the instructions.

That was easy for him to say. He barely spoke English.

I think they're planning a takeover.

Are We Really This Stupid?
(Sept. 20, 1987)

Most Americans believe that they belong to one of the most intelligent and best-educated societies in the world.

They don't.

This revelation came to me as a result of a recent shopping trip.

Silly me, I always thought the people of the most powerful nation on earth were capable of making it through the day without outside help. There would always be those who would have trouble concentrating and breathing at the same time, of course, but the population as a whole had always struck me as being of at least average mental ability.

It took that shopping trip to make me realize how wrong I was.

The source of inspiration was my daughter's new hair crimper.

The directions that accompanied it included the usual safety warnings – "unplug after using, keep away from water, do not leave unattended," etc.

Then the thunderbolt:

"DO NOT CRIMP HAIR WHILE SLEEPING."

Sleeping?

They couldn't be serious. What kind of pinhead would try to use a hair crimper (or any other electrical appliance) while sleeping?

Presently it occurred to me that they were serious. If you think about who writes safety instructions, it makes sense. The people who write safety instructions are lawyers, whose job is to assure that every conceivable hazard is spelled out, getting the manufacturers off the hook in case of a lawsuit.

That means that somewhere in this country is a firm of well-educated, successful, presumably bright attorneys, who believe that there are people witless enough to injure themselves while trying to crimp their hair in their sleep. Worse, they believe there are enough of them to justify warnings in safety manuals.

Impossible? Look at the Iowa Republican straw vote.

Curious, I began to check the instructions on other household items.

The directions for my electric razor were relatively conventional (unplug before cleaning, do not use with damaged plug, etc.) with the exception of No. 2:

"Do not use in the shower."

Of course! Who hasn't experienced a frantic desire to jump in the shower with an electric razor, turn on the water and razor at the same time, and be transformed into a memorial fountain? I've suffered from this obsession for years. Only my superior intelligence has allowed me to rise above it.

The same goes for the package of silica gel I recently encountered in a shoebox. Printed on the package were a skull and crossbones and the words "Do not eat."

It's a good thing that warning was there, or I'd have devoured the package and its contents on the spot. Silica gel is one of my favorite delicacies, along with floppy disks and Styrofoam packing balls.

My favorite set of directions came with a portable radio. The first instruction – "read instructions." Next, "retain instructions." Having read and retained the instructions, the owner is instructed to "heed instructions." Then (just in case), he is warned to "follow instructions."

A presidential contender recently was quoted as saying the country "lacked direction."

He must not be able to read.

The Voicemail Monster
(Oct. 15, 1992)

"Hello, I have a question about a bill. I was wondering …"

"If you are calling our administrative offices, please press 1."

The voice belonged to a computer. Like countless other frustrated Americans, I had become a victim of the most irritating phenomenon of the information age – voicemail.

"If you are calling our technical division, please press 2."

"I don't want to talk to your technical division. I want …"

"If you are calling our accounting division, press 3."

I pressed 3. An accountant wasn't what I had in mind, but it beat talking to a computer.

"Hello, is this accounting?"

"If your question is about an account opened in the last 90 days, press 1."

"But I don't want to press 1. All I want to do is ask a simple question. Is my bill …"

"If your question is about a delinquent account, press 2."

The question, if there had been anyone to listen to it, was whether a bill had been paid. Neither my wife nor I could find it in our records. The account might have been a tad overdue, but it certainly wasn't delinquent. A person would have understood that. A computer only understands numbers.

What to do? If I pressed 2, would the computer label me a deadbeat? Would hairy men with tire irons come in the night? Was there a Turkish prison in my future? I began to feel hot and clammy. I did nothing.

"If your question is about the meaning of life, press 3."

The computer didn't really say that, I made it up. But it raises some fascinating voicemail possibilities, don't you think?

"If your question is about National League baseball playoffs, press 4."

"If your question is about missing socks in your laundry, press 5."

"If your question is about a current billing, press 6."

Finally! I pressed 6.

"Please press your 12-digit account number now."

I did.

"This is not a valid account number. If you live west of the Mississippi River, press 1."

I pressed 1. Hard.

"If you live north of the Platte River, press 1."

Technology is supposed to simplify our lives, right? So when was the last time (before voicemail) that you needed an atlas to find out whether a bill had been paid?

Or a translator. Last week I had to call a government office simplified by the wonders of voicemail. There was no way my questions could be answered by computer, but that's all I ever got. I made it through the triple-digit responses, but gave up when it started speaking Spanish.

For bureaucrats and others who can't be bothered by calls from the public, voicemail is a time saver. They're the ones whose lives it simplifies. For the rest of us, it can be about as time saving as a straitjacket.

But I've strayed from our story.

After the computer decided which river I lived on, it asked me to enter my ZIP code. I must have goofed, because, after ruminating on it, the computer declared my ZIP code an "invalid option. If you need assistance, please press 0."

I don't want to press anything!" I shrieked. "I want to talk to a REAL PERSON!"

At this point, we will draw the curtain of mercy over this episode, except to say that the computer finally spat out the desired response.

"Your account is paid in full."

It took 12 minutes. A human could have handled it in two.

Airport Hell
(Feb. 3, 2005)

SPOKANE — I'm writing this in the Spokane airport. I don't ever want to see the Spokane airport again. Or any other airport.

It's 5:30 a.m. I've been traveling for 39 hours and counting. I'm wearing the same clothes I wore yesterday, have had seven hours of sleep in the last 48, and if anyone says "fogged in" again, I'm going to set my ticket on fire and hitchhike.

The trip began in Key West, Fla., where a friend and I went for a wedding. We skipped dinner after the wedding to drive to Fort Lauderdale, where we had an early flight home the next morning. This proved to be a serious error. Except for a tuna-fish sandwich in Key West and a taco in Houston, I've been living on airline peanuts for two days.

It looked like such an easy trip. Our itinerary said we were going from Fort Lauderdale to Houston to L.A. to Boise. My friend Mac, who lives in Coeur d'Alene, would spend the night in Boise and fly to Spokane the next morning.

The first surprise was ... Orlando! It wasn't on the itinerary or even mentioned until we were boarding the plane.

The second surprise happened in Houston. That's where we learned that our plane was continuing on to L.A. without us. We'd conveniently been booked for an L.A. connection three and a half hours later — even though our plane had empty seats and could have connected with flights that would have had us home for dinner. It was at this point I began to suspect that our travel agent was the same person who synchronizes Boise's traffic lights.

The third surprise was another unannounced stop. After watching the wind blow in Houston for three and a half hours and flying to L.A. to catch what we thought was a direct flight to Boise, we were now going to ... Reno!

No, as a matter of fact it wasn't on the itinerary, either. It was also fogged in.

Skimming mountains on a foggy, inky night may be some people's idea of fun, but it isn't mine and it definitely wasn't Mac's. He looked like he was going to spontaneously combust.

We circled and circled some more, waiting for the happy announcement that we could forget Reno and continue on to Boise. That's when we got surprise No. 4 — Oakland!

Oakland was where the Reno passengers deplaned, leaving seven of us with our personal 737 to Boise. It was kind of nice, actually, right up until surprise No. 5.

Boise was fogged in. Then we were going to ... Spokane!

Mac was thrilled. That's where he wanted to go all along. It's also where our flight was scheduled to terminate, but for reasons known only to the airline gods he'd been booked to go there from Boise the next day. Now he'd be home early — a happy, if exhausted, man.

I, on the other hand, got to flop on an airport motel bed at 1 a.m. and get up four tossing-and-turning hours later. My flight to Boise was scheduled to leave at 6:45 a.m. It would have, too, except for surprise No. 6. Boise was still fogged in.

I honestly expected to finish writing this in Boise, or at least on a plane bound for Boise. Instead, I'm still in Spokane and may be here till spring. The 6:45 flight was canceled, the 10:15 was canceled and the next scheduled flight isn't until evening, when the fog will be even thicker.

Our would-be captain told me a lot of airports have landing systems that allow planes to land in fog as thick as axle grease.

Boise isn't one of those airports.

So here I am, two days and counting. My itinerary reads like an atlas — Key West, Ft. Lauderdale, Orlando, Houston, L.A., Reno, Oakland, Boise and Spokane — where I may perish. The restaurants were closed when we landed last night and, except for a snack bar pushing coronary sludge, closed when I got here this morning. I'm hungry, my back hurts from sitting in plastic torture units, my eyes are burning slits and if I ever get home I'm going to write the airline and tell them what I think of their sneaky habit of throwing in cities that aren't on the itinerary.

I think somebody should look into getting Boise one of those fancy landing systems, too.

Not that it matters to me. From now on, I'm driving. It's not as safe as flying, but it's faster.

Airport Hell II
(March 3, 2005)

I'm never driving to an airport again. I know; in a recent column on being fogged out of Boise I vowed never to fly again. This time was different, though. My son and I were merely dropping off my wife at the airport. I wouldn't be setting so much as a big toe inside. What could possibly go wrong?

Well, let me tell you.

Against my better judgment, we decided to take our dog, Molly, along for the ride. I've long suspected that Molly is a reincarnation of Benedict Arnold, but that's another story. We stopped in the "departures" area, got the bags out of the trunk and said goodbye. The car was in the park-at-risk-of-lethal-injection zone, so we made it quick. Then I started to get back in the car.

That's when we noticed the problem. The car was locked.

That should have been impossible. You can't lock the car without the keys, and the keys were still in the ignition.

You know how it is when something happens that can't happen? You stare stupidly at the evidence that it has and mutter inanities like "Thiscan'tbehappenin'!" and "Who-eee!" That's how it was — until we realized what happened.

Our dog had locked us out of the car!

The culprit was goofily grinning from the console, which has a lock button I'd forgotten existed. Molly had stepped on the button and was clearly delighted with herself. (She really does grin.) This is a dog that took a year to house train, knocks over every wastebasket in the house, chews the furniture, throws up at the worst possible times and places, bites family members and welcomes prospective burglars.

This time, she'd outdone herself. The car wasn't far from the spot where, after leaving it for a few heartbeats once while trying to spot someone I was picking up, an officer presented me with a $100 ticket. It's arguably the worst place in Idaho to be locked out of your car.

Do you think we could get the dog to step on the button again and open the car? Do you think we could find a cop to ask for help? No, and no again. The cop who'd ticketed me faster than a fly on honey was nowhere to be seen, and the dog who had locked the car in a nanosecond lay there like a contented slug. She hadn't had this much fun since she was a pup.

The woman from the auto club wanted to know the number on my card, the address and telephone number at the home I was locked out of, the nearest cross streets to the airport (she was most likely in India), the year, make, model and color of my vehicle, the kind of transmission ... It was a nasty February day with a double-digit wind chill, we were flirting with hypothermia, a SWAT team would be arriving momentarily to incinerate the car — and she wanted to play 20 questions.

Here we'll draw the curtain over this adventure, except to say that a locksmith eventually arrived and got us into the car. She said it was the most stubborn lock she'd ever seen.

By the time we got home from the airport, a distance of maybe three miles, my wife was having dinner with her sister in Seattle.

The dog?

She's on medication now. A skin problem. My guess is she's allergic to upholstery.

The good news is the vet says she'll be fine. And she's really not a bad dog. She knows a trick, kids love her, and though she's a bit long in the tooth (she has several of those), people still mistake her for a puppy.

Did I mention that she's free to a good home?

Idaho's Siberia
(Jan. 7, 1993)

With the arrival of Idaho's first real winter in years, the hot topic in ice-encrusted towns from Three Creek to Good Grief is the lost art of winter driving.

Idahoans long have prided themselves on their ability to handle vehicles careening over icy roads at speeds that reduce ordinary motorists to nerve endings. This, after all, is Rocky Mountain country. If you can't handle winter, move to some wimpy Sunbelt state.

The drought changed all that. Its snowless winters made us complacent. Our winter-driving skills languished.

Now we're paying the price, as I learned during a recent trip to Idaho Falls. That a native Boisean would even consider going to Idaho Falls at this time of year is an indication of the extent to which the drought has addled our brains. When tulips are blooming in Boise, Idaho Falls is having ice storms. It is a highly wintry place.

Blithely ignoring this, I set out for the tundras of eastern Idaho. My one concession to the winter driving tips inundating the news reports was a well-aged but never-used set of chains.

At Burley, the interstate became a ribbon of ice with ruts deep enough to lose a Winnebago. It was like driving on a very narrow glacier. After passing several cars that had hurtled off the freeway and buried themselves in snow, I stopped and asked a trucker whether the road ahead was any better.

"Where you going?" he asked.

"Idaho Falls."

"That's where I came from," he said. "If you think this is bad, wait until you get to Pocatello."

Thus encouraged, I pressed on to Pocatello at the dizzying speed of 40 mph. The car would have gone off the road a dozen times if not for the relentless attentions of my white, aching knuckles on the wheel. It was an unbelievably grueling drive. And this was the easy part.

Just north of Pocatello, the ruts gave way to a gleaming sheet of ice over which someone, probably the devil, had spread bearing grease. Traffic barely moved. I crept to Fort Hall, slid into a truck stop and asked a State Police officer his views on the subject of chains.

"Well, we've had 150 slideoffs in the next 40 miles," he said. "I'd say chains are a good idea."

If you know how to put them on. I didn't. Neither did two truckers, whom I offered money, the rest of my tuna-salad sandwich and the deed to my house. I was lying on the ice under my car, cursing, when a woman stopped and began to curse her chains. She said she was going home to Blackfoot.

"That's only 14 miles."

"I'm not going one more mile in this!" she said. "I slid off and have been hit tonight already. I'm calling my husband."

Her husband, a mechanical type and an incredibly nice guy, drove down from Blackfoot and had both cars ready to go in no time. With chains, I was able to slip and slide the rest of the way at 25 mph. It was the eeriest drive I've ever made.

Every minute or so, a slideoff would appear in the headlights, ghostlike, buried to its windows in drifting snow. Time and again, flares and emergency lights illuminated shrouded figures stranded in the night. At a rest stop, a semi had crossed the median strip, flipped onto its side and plunged over an embankment. Traffic slowed to 20 mph.

The trip took eight hours. You can get to Hawaii faster than that. As the wheels crunched to a stop, I made a solemn promise.

The next time I go to Idaho Falls in the winter will be when taxes go down, the sun rises in the West and the Cubs are in the World Series.

Cruising? No Thanks.
(April 6, 2006)

Every few years, my wife and I take a splurge vacation. That's a vacation you can't afford but take anyway because it's more fun than, say, scraping paint or visiting the relatives.

This time last week, we were cruising the coast of Central America. We figured a cruise would be something different, we got a great deal on the Internet, and the image of sailing to exotic places and lounging on sunny tropical beaches was hard to resist.

The ship left from exotic La Porte, Texas. La Porte is part of the Houston shipyard-railroad-oil refinery megaplex, an industrial blight so vast and surpassingly ugly it's hard to believe it isn't New Jersey. The cruise was discounted after being moved there from storm-ravaged New Orleans, and after seeing Houston it wasn't hard to see why. We checked our luggage for unwanted souvenirs — sludge, noxious weeds, toxic chemicals — and gratefully boarded the ship.

I was sick within an hour.

It was the dreaded Woodward Vacation Illness Curse. The next two days were a blur of fever, nausea and aching muscles — and we weren't even in Mexico yet.

By the time we did get to Mexico, I was feeling well enough to limp along while my wife shopped. Men may say they go to Mexico to drink tequila and parasail, but it's a lie. We're really just beasts of burden.

Let me say right here that my wife is a wonderful woman with many fine qualities. She's kind, generous, has a marvelous sense of humor and is way smarter than the guy who lugs her packages around for her. On the other hand, 2,000 people can descend simultaneously from a ship and the street vendors will ignore 1,999 of them to focus on her alone — the Holy Grail of shoppers. If you'd care to know the best places to buy anything from conch shells to mahogany notepad holders, and the preferred methods of packing and hauling them, I'm your guy.

The next day was reserved for the beach. The prospect of lying in a deck chair on a quiet beach with the tropical sun baking winter from our bones had sustained me through the months of paying off the cruise balances on the credit card. But it wasn't to be.

Answer this if you can: What is it about human beings that makes them think that nothing in nature, no matter how serene or beautiful, can fail to be improved by the addition of powerful speakers playing music that is almost supernaturally annoying? What's wrong with the sound of the surf? We'd barely wet our toes when someone switched on a zillion watts of computer music, the sonic equivalent of having a spike driven through your forehead.

Then it started to rain. Not a warm tropical rain, but a chilling, wind-driven downpour. Foolishly having neglected to bring our Sorrels or parkas, we spent the rest of the day shivering in swimsuits under a sodden beach umbrella, drinking frightfully expensive beer and listening to Ziggy and the Cyber Jackhammers.

A woman who worked at the beach warned us about sand fleas.

"They don't bother most people, " she said. "But those they do, they just about drive crazy."

Sand fleas are little black bugs that sting like crazy. You don't pay much attention until you get home, start scratching and can't stop. The woman at the beach was right, though; they don't bother most people. The greatest number of bites anyone else reported was two. My tally, at last count: 43.

Did I mention post-cruise disorder? That's the inner ear's way of getting even for being subjected to a week at sea. Home for four days now, we're dizzy about half the time and wake up in the night with the bed rolling on a ship that isn't there. The computer screen is rolling as I write this, and I'm spending an alarming amount of time lurching into everything from furniture to startled colleagues.

People have asked whether we'd ever want to take another cruise. As a matter of fact, I'm already planning a cruise to visit an old friend. He lives in exotic North Idaho.

Elvis Goes Berserk
(Sept. 10, 2007)

One of the last things a happily married person expects is to be caught in a love triangle, but it happened to me during a recent assignment.

The members of the threesome were myself, a woman named Andrea Zollweg and my rival for her affection.

His name is Elvis.

Elvis is an exceptionally formidable individual. In fact, his jealousy over my relationship with Zollweg erupted with such intensity that if he hadn't been locked up I'd have feared for my life.

The fact that Elvis is a spider monkey is beside the point.

You probably saw Zollweg's picture on the front page of the Statesman a week ago. Photographer Joe Jaszewski and I spent time with her and other workers for a Labor Day story about people who do what some would consider dirty jobs. As part of her job as a zookeeper at Zoo Boise, Zollweg has to clean up after the animals.

That's where we met my volatile rival. Joe, who got to the zoo ahead of me and was photographing Zollweg when I unsuspectingly stepped into the monkey cage, later admitted that he'd had the benefit of an advance warning.

"They said I shouldn't even look him in the eye, " Joe said. "I didn't dare raise a camera to him."

There wasn't time for him to say that in the cage, however. All he managed to get out was a whispered, "Don't make eye contact!"

No eye contact? Why wouldn't I make eye contact with an interview subject? Zollweg didn't look intimidating. In fact, she seemed just the opposite. A friendlier, more cheerful person would have been hard to imagine.

"Good morning," I said, reaching to shake her hand. "I'm Tim Wood..."

That's when the room exploded. Elvis leaped onto the cage door, clenching its wire grate with his fingers and toes and shaking it so violently I thought the hinges would tear loose. His body rocked back and forth like Richard Simmons on amphetamines. I was about a yard away with my back to him when he launched the attack and had no idea it was coming.

It's only a slight exaggeration to say that I came out of my skin. I may even have temporarily lost the power of speech. But I categorically deny wetting my pants.

As if hurling himself against the cage door wasn't enough, Elvis was shrieking like a deranged "American Idol" contestant.

"I'm going to have nightmares about this," Joe said, looking shaken.

"Is he always like this?" I asked Zollweg.

Impossible as it seemed, that made Elvis even angrier. He slammed himself against the cage door with such demonic fury that we'd have been justified in calling an exorcist. Forgetting Joe's advice, I briefly made eye contact.

Two things about that were unnerving. One was that Elvis' eyes were a psychotically vibrant shade of blue. The other was that they seethed with hatred. Every fiber of his being was focused on annihilating me.

There wasn't the slightest doubt that if he'd gotten out — and the wires of the cage door suddenly looked way too flimsy — he'd have finished me off in less time than it takes a pit bull to finish a Slim Jim.

"I'm going to have nightmares about this," Joe repeated.

Elvis calmed down a bit when we left the cage for the visitors' area, where Zollweg revealed the shocking truth.

"I've worked here long enough that he thinks I'm part of his harem," she said.

"Harem? You're joking."

"No. He sees you as competition. Watch this."

She put her hand on my shoulder for about half a second, long enough for Elvis to erupt in another gymnastic fit of rage.

Asked how he and her husband got along, Zollweg smiled playfully and said, "My husband doesn't know about me and Elvis."

At that point we opted to go outside, ostensibly to watch her and a coworker clean the "rain forest." Actually I wanted to put as much distance as possible between myself and the glowering monkey, who smoldered and watched our progress while conversing with the other spider monkeys. My guess is he was bargaining for some wire cutters, or possibly an AK-47.

I left the zoo that day with a feeling of limitless gratitude for the designers of the cage door that had protected me from Elvis. True, he's just a spider monkey, not a lion or a tiger or even a baboon. But never have I witnessed anything like his all-out, murderous wrath. Compared with that, lions and tigers seem almost gentle.

Later, Zollweg told me Elvis' age. He's 40, which is ancient for a spider monkey.

An old man, in other words, long past his prime.

I think I'm going to have nightmares about this.

Chrysler's Improbable Savior
(June 7, 2009)

As the former owner of a Fiat, I've been following the proposed Chrysler-Fiat merger with disbelief bordering on the surreal.

If my car was representative, asking Fiat to throw Chrysler a rope is like asking Dick Cheney to teach a hunter-safety course.

A Fiat was the first new car my wife and I ever owned. Neither of us will ever forget it. Newlyweds at the time, we'd taken a cheap university flight to Europe and had to buy a car that would get us around on our honeymoon and follow us home to a new life.

In one corner was a blue Volkswagen Bug. I'd owned several used bugs and liked them. Not exciting, maybe, but solid and dependable. The German sausage of cars. A solid choice.

In the other corner was a cherry red, Fiat sport coupe. Low, sleek, sexy — and cheap. Neither of us knew a thing about Fiats, except that we had to have one. Like a tempting Italian pastry, it seduced us.

It's an understatement to say that it was fun to drive. It took corners like they didn't exist. In a way, it reminded me of my first car, an ancient MG that cost $400 to buy and another $400 to keep running for a year. What I didn't know at the time was that the Fiat was the MG's wicked, possibly deranged Italian cousin.

The first clue that our new car lacked the reliability I'd taken for granted in Bugs came at a campground in Germany. "When it comes to art, the Italians think of everything," I said. "Look at the way those beautiful silver rings on the tires catch the glow of the campfire."

Closer examination showed that the rings weren't artwork. They were steel belts poking through the rubber. Our new car had gone less than 2,000 miles and the back tires were shot.

The next set gave out in about 1,500 miles. The problem, we were told, was that the rear wheels had to be aligned. And the second you drove over anything of substance —a curb, a pebble, a piece of pasta — they were out of whack again.

"Fill it up?" gas station attendants would ask.

"No. Just check the gas and change the tires."

We were breaking in our third set of tires when the car caught fire. So much smoke was pouring from the engine compartment you'd have thought we had a Thanksgiving turkey in it.

The problem this time was the battery. No one had told us it needed frequent infusions of distilled water. "Fill it up, sir?"

"Yes. Fill up the battery and change the tires."

We were driving down a road in Italy when one of the side mirrors fell off and smashed on the pavement. Then the strangest thing of all happened. The car began to howl like a sick animal. Not regularly, but every now and then, when you least expected it. A mournful, almost human-sounding wail. It was eerie.

Worried that it could be something else about to fall off, wear out or burn up, we stopped and asked about it at an Italian service garage.

"What kind of car is it?" the man at the desk asked.

"A Fiat."

"A Fiat? Take it to Germany."

"But it's an Italian car!"

"Yes, but the best mechanics are in Germany."

When it was time to ship the car home, my wife was understandably emotional.

"Drive it off the pier," she said.

"What?"

"Drive it off the pier. Sink it. I never want to see this stupid car again."

We took it home, of course — we couldn't afford to sink it — and endured a year of shredded tires, ghostly howls and malfunctioning everything before selling it cheap. When the buyers drove it away, we cheered and did cartwheels.

I hope Fiat has come far since then. I really do. I hope the cars it makes with Chrysler will save jobs, revive the economy and boost the stock market.

Tip: you might want to invest in some companies that make tires.

A Perfect, Paint-Free World
(June 28, 2009)

Someday in a better world, people will have alternatives to the things that frustrate us today.

They'll have conquered gravity, harnessed the sun and achieved world peace.

And if they're really lucky, they'll have invented an alternative to paint.

This came to me after cleaning up a nasty — and almost diabolically persistent — paint spill.

And I hadn't even been painting.

The paint was left over from a room painted months earlier. I know you're not supposed to put paint cans in the trash and am borderline-obsessive about taking them to the fire station for disposal. But this can was all but empty. It couldn't have had more than a thimbleful of paint, which I assumed had dried up.

Wrong. The value of one of the first rules of journalism — never assume — was reaffirmed by a voicemail left by my wife the early riser while on her way to work.

"An animal knocked over our trash," she said. "I cleaned it up the best I could. Except for the paint."

Sure enough, the "thimbleful of dried-up paint" had made a mess of shocking proportions on the front sidewalk.

Have you ever noticed that when you're trying to finish a project and only have a small amount of paint, it's never enough? But just try spilling it. What won't cover a square foot on a wall can make a stain the size of a wading pool on your new hardwood floor.

Wondering how such a small amount of paint could stain such a large amount of sidewalk, I began the cleanup.

After half an hour or so of repeated blotting with paper towels, vigorous scrubbing with a wire brush and high-pressure spray from a garden hose, the sidewalk looked almost normal.

It's a good thing Roadmaster wasn't there to see it. Roadmaster was a railroad tramp immortalized by the late Utah Phillips. One of the rules he lived by was, "Never have anything you have to feed or paint." You wouldn't have caught him scrubbing paint off some stupid sidewalk.

Late for work by this time, I took the can back to the garage to get rid of later. That's when I realized that the can had a small crack in one side and had leaked more paint, on the sidewalk and the garage floor.

At about the same time, my daughter appeared on the scene — drawn, perhaps, by the sound of spirited cursing.

"What's wrong?" she asked.

"This #%*! paint can. It was empty and now it's spewing paint like Old Faithful. If it was food instead of paint, we could use it to end world hunger."

Trying to help, she grabbed the can and watched in dismay as it dribbled paint onto the trash-can lid and her new pants and jacket.

Where was the stuff coming from? True, the paint obviously wasn't dried up, but the can really did look virtually empty.

"Stay here," I told her. "I'll go inside and get some more paper towels."

That meant walking across the sidewalk and front porch, through the entryway and across the kitchen.

By now you've guessed that in addition to being nearly everywhere else, there was paint on the bottoms of my shoes.

And the kitchen floor, the entryway floor, the porch. All from a supposedly empty can of dried-up paint.

That night, I made a deal with God. If I ever put another paint can in the trash instead of taking it to the fire station, He (or She, depending on one's gender convictions) can strike me dead.

Conquering gravity and harnessing the sun are all right. World peace would be even better.

But in a really perfect world, there won't be paint.

A Bite Out of Government?
(Nov. 15, 1992)

Wanted: responsible person for office work. $100,000-plus salary. Benefits include $4,600 monthly pension, adjusted annually for inflation.

Twenty years ago, in a tavern in North Idaho, congressional candidate Steve Symms lectured an audience consisting of a bartender and rookie reporter on the evils of "Potomac Fever."

Potomac Fever was defined as the affliction that caused newcomers to Congress to become entrenched in the Washington political system. It was capable of turning even the most well-meaning reformer into a professional politician. The antidote was to limit oneself to two terms.

I remember the conversation because I was the rookie reporter. My boss had sent me to Kellogg to follow up on an accident that had killed 92 miners there earlier that year. In my spare time, I was to cover the North Idaho exploits of a different kind of congressional candidate – young, colorful, brimming with folksy slogans attacking big government.

Four House and two Senate terms later, it could be argued that the young reformer himself succumbed to a touch of Potomac Fever.

Those who have followed his war on big government could hardly fail to miss the irony in last week's disclosure of Sen. Symms' projected pension figures.

Was this what the young candidate meant, all those years ago, when he promised to "take a bite out of government?"

The final bite, for those who missed it, is $4,637 a month. That's the starting figure. With cost of living adjustments, it will end up being even more. Based on his life expectancy, Symms is expected to receive more than $2.7 million in retirement payments.

Most lottery winners don't get that much.

Would you be interested in a job that paid $129,000 a year, gave you extended holidays, the entire month of August and every fourth week off, and allowed you to retire after 20 years with a starting pension more than three times the state's average per capita income?

Of course you would. Only a millionaire or a couch potato wouldn't be interested in a job with those kinds of benefits.

Not that Symms is doing anything his colleagues aren't doing. There's no law against cashing in on the system. The problem is the system's fading line between public service and the public trough.

Real public service is a sacrifice. Traditionally, it's been the citizen's way of paying back the community. If the community was good to you, you repaid the debt by working for a time at a public post. The pay was negligible, the job an imposition.

Today, we tend to see that mostly at the lowest levels of government (zoning boards, irrigation districts, etc.). At the higher levels, candidates spend millions campaigning and otherwise clawing their way into jobs that bear little resemblance to the traditional concept of public service.

It would be surprising if they didn't. Most of the money they spend isn't their own, and a few terms of "public service" can set the winners up for life.

In the campaign just-ended, nearly all of the candidates talked about the need to reduce the federal deficit. But how many campaigned for reform of bloated federal pensions, now two to three times greater than their counterparts in private industry?

One candidate had a name for the problem 20 years ago.

He called it Potomac Fever.

GOP Award Blurs Line Between Right, Wrong
(Feb. 12, 1987)

I must have missed something.

Perhaps I blinked during American Government class, or skipped an important political science lecture. Whatever the reason, I have been able to spend my adult life in abysmal ignorance of the workings of the American political system.

Silly me, I always thought that our political system was based on noble principles that were meant to foster the qualities and values that Americans admire.

Even after Watergate and other lapses, I regarded most politicians as public-spirited individuals who, despite the occasional lunatics in their midst, aspired to keep and protect those values, to practice them in their own lives and preserve them for future generations.

Politics was the art of public service. The political parties were dedicated to providing the best leaders and public servants they could, and to upholding the principles on which the country was founded. At their best, the political parties encouraged statesmanship, and produced statesmen.

Enter George Hansen and the Republican Party of Idaho.

Hansen, according to a recent news story, will be honored Friday by GOP leaders in eastern Idaho. The former congressman, the story reported, will be the recipient of "a special award" during the Republican Party's annual Lincoln's Day banquet in Idaho Falls.

This, for the benefit of newcomers to the state or readers with short memories, is the same George Hansen who was released in December from a federal prison. That he has needed less than two months to go from jail to the awards table is a testimony to his staying power and to the willingness of his party to accommodate diversity. One minute a prison inmate, the next an honored guest at a prestigious political function.

This is the same George Hansen who was convicted of failing to report more than $330,000 in financial transactions while serving as a member of Congress.

That may not sound like a lot of money in terms of the figures Congress is accustomed to working with, but it's more than most Idahoans make in a decade.

Yet this is the same George Hansen who invariably seemed to be in financial trouble, the man who considered himself qualified to help run the affairs of the nation while his wife publicly solicited donations to bail him out of his financial emergencies.

This is the same George Hansen who, in addition to being the first congressman ever imprisoned for violating the Ethics in Government Act, was sentenced a decade earlier to two years in prison (reduced to a $2,000 fine) for failing to file an adequate campaign finance report.

The same George Hansen who flew to Iran to single-handedly rescue the American hostages there, the same George Hansen who was more than six months late filing his 1975 tax return, the same George Hansen whose own campaign depicted him as a character in a comic book.

The people of the 2nd Congressional District could be forgiven if they had difficulty deciding whether their congressman was a statesman or, to borrow from his campaign literature, something out of the funny papers.

Now, fresh from the slammer, Hansen is to be honored by the Republican Party.

Which says something about honor in politics.

A GOP official said the former congressman deserved the award for his running battles against the federal government, particularly the Internal Revenue Service and the Justice Department.

If that's the standard, perhaps we should give an award to Claude Dallas. Talk about running battles with the federal government! Dallas has been giving the feds the fits – running and battling, battling and running. And if George can get a fancy dinner and a special award for it, Claude deserves at least a certificate of merit.

On the other hand, Dallas has been close-mouthed about his civic life.

Perhaps he isn't interested in political honors.

As far as that goes, he might not even be a Republican.

Responsible Republicans, those who truly believe in the guiding principles of their party, must be outraged by the way some of their leaders are planning to observe the birth of its greatest statesman.

But the real outrage of the Lincoln's Day tribute to Hansen is the message it sends to the people of Idaho, particularly its young people.

In honoring such a man, the Republican Party is blurring the line between right and wrong.

If an elected official can commit a crime and be sentenced to prison only to get out and be treated like a hero, what incentive is there for anyone else to respect the law?

Our Bird-Brained Quarter
(Aug. 4, 2005)

Idaho's state quarter. (Idaho Statesman file photo)

Dear Gov. Kempthorne: A recent news story said you were looking for ideas for Idaho's state quarter.

You're going to get a truckload of them, meaning the hardest part of your job will be to eliminate ideas. Those already submitted include everything from a finger steak to a "No Vacancy" sign.

As a lifelong Idahoan who has spent years writing about the state, I'd like to offer some suggestions on how to narrow the field:

The first thing to reject is any idea using a geographic outline. So many states have used them on their coins that they're already a cliché. And state outlines are about as visually interesting as dirt.

The second thing to lose is the quarter by committee. That's what happens when a committee can't choose from a lot of so-so ideas and ends up using all of them.

We're talking a one-inch circle here, governor. That's not a lot of room for one work of art, let alone a hodgepodge of them. A hodgepodge is what happened in Minnesota, whose quarter features the state's nickname, the state outline, a tree-lined lake, two people fishing from a boat, and a loon.

South Carolina's is even worse. It has the state nickname, the dreaded outline, a palmetto tree, the state bird, the state flower and a star for the state capital. If they'd had another eighth-inch, they'd have crammed in a plantation house and a bowl of grits.

Forget boats, too. Boats are all right, but they're overdone. Rhode Island has a sailboat, Virginia a fleet of sailboats, Minnesota a fishing boat, Missouri a riverboat, Florida a galleon ... Someone is sure to suggest a jet boat, drift boat or kayak, but why be like all those other states? Our quarter should be unique.

Don't even think about using a map. Maps are even more boring than state outlines. It's hard to believe that civic leaders working for months on designs couldn't think of anything more appealing than eyestrain-inducing maps, but that's what happened in Michigan and Louisiana. Michigan's quarter has a map of the Great Lakes, Louisiana's of the Louisiana Purchase. The state that gave us Creole and Cajun culture, Mardi Gras and Tabasco Sauce, and the most interesting thing they can think of is a map?

You're going to get scads of suggestions for lakes, rivers, mountains, plants, animals and people. Many will have merit. The trouble, especially with choosing people, comes in trying to pick just one. I can't think of a single Idahoan, living or dead, who so towers above all others that he or she should represent the state on a coin.

The same is true of places. How do you choose between Redfish Lake and Lake Pend Oreille? The Sawtooths or Mount Borah? My choice would be a generic Idaho scene, something showing our spectacular mountains and maybe a whitewater river. Throw in a raptor flying overhead and call it good.

My opinion isn't important, though. The important thing is that whatever you choose portrays Idaho as the beautiful state it is and doesn't reinforce its undeserved stereotypes. Pick whatever you want, governor, as long as it reflects the Idaho we know and love.

All of this is a long way of leading up to my main point. We all know what our diverse and wonderful state is known for, and it's time to change that narrow-minded image. Enlightened Idahoans everywhere are hoping you'll do something about this sensitive issue.

Please, Governor, in the name of all we hold dear about our state, in the cherished hope that others will see us in a progressive light...

Heavy on the mountains, hold the spuds.

Medicaid Helps More People Than You Think
(March 20, 2011)

You might think that Idaho's Medicaid cuts will only apply to "other people."

People you don't know and never will. Certainly not you, your friends or anyone in your family.

Wrong. Those people are in families from Bear Lake to Bonners Ferry. Countless Idahoans are all too familiar with the reasons that force people to rely on Medicaid.

My family, for example. For us, the reason is mental illness. I've never written about it before because I didn't want to embarrass any family members. But I checked with them and they're OK with it. And if ever the subject was timely, it's now.

The first, as far as we know, was my mother. When she was in her 70s, her behavior went from eccentric to alarming.

She was sure people were stealing from her. She was distant with one of our daughters and fawned over the other, who called one night to say her grandmother had taken her on a plane ride. They were in a strange airport and didn't know what to do. The airport was in San Francisco.

When my father got so sick he almost died, her response was to tell him she couldn't stand being around sick people. It was her mental illness talking, but he took it to heart. She may or may not have suggested that he move out — we were never sure about that — but either way, he did. They stayed married, but he spent the rest of his life living alone in an apartment.

Deeply religious, she became convinced that a monk had fallen in love with her and they were going to be married. A woman who had always cared about appearances, she caused a minor sensation one night by building a shrine in her front yard. One of her neighbors called me at 3 a.m. to report that his once proper neighbor, wearing only her nightgown, was sitting in a lawn chair surrounded by candles and crucifixes.

Carrying your mother kicking and screaming to a mental hospital isn't something you can feel good about, but it was necessary. She got the help she needed and was more or less stable for the rest of her life.

The next family member was our son. It took a succession of doctors and most of his childhood to get a final diagnosis: a form of schizophrenia. His intelligence was above average, but his illness interfered with his thought processes. He'd stay up all night doing homework most kids finished by bedtime. No one tried harder, or struggled against greater odds.

People with mental illnesses pay a heavy price emotionally. He was 16 when he threatened to kill himself with a butcher knife. The officers who responded were cool-headed enough to talk him into dropping it, but the situation could have escalated to the point they felt their only option was to use force. Our son could easily have died that day.

Today, he's doing much better. He's a talented artist, a hard worker, a good person. He has a job and lives independently. You won't find a steadier, more responsible person. Medicaid helped make that possible. It covers counseling and medications he could never afford on his own.

The family illness, meanwhile, is now in its third generation. Our 11-year old grandson recently was diagnosed with a form of autism. He's getting the help he needs from Medicaid, too.

In one case, Medicaid has meant the difference between normalcy and something else, possibly between life and death. In the other, it means a shot at a relatively normal life.

Without Medicaid, who knows? I try not to think about that because the possibilities are too terrible.

People with developmental disabilities, a mental health care professional told me, "need all the help they can get to stay balanced and out of hospitals. Medicine and a few hours' of therapy a month are a good deal compared to hospitals that costs thousands a day."

Thousands saved, incidentally, in taxes.

Help from programs like Medicaid are what an enlightened society does for those who weren't born as lucky as the rest of us. It doesn't just apply to "other people." It helps us all.

2500 Lemp Street
(April 5, 2009)

You never know when something will unearth buried memories, transporting you in an instant to another time.

It happened to me recently while reading an Ask Tim email. Most Ask Tim emails have fairly conventional subject lines, but this one was the address of my childhood home in North Boise. It was from a woman named Valerie, who lives there now, and who said she was mystified by the living-room fireplace. This was hardly surprising; the fireplace mystified my family for all the years we lived there.

"We simply cannot figure out how to make a fire in the fireplace without gassing ourselves silly," Valerie wrote. "Any tricks that you remember working?"

Apparently she and her husband had all but succumbed to smoke inhalation. I couldn't be of much help, having almost succumbed to smoke inhalation in virtually every place I've ever lived that had a fireplace. To me, fireplaces are like personal computers, endlessly fickle and reliably infuriating.

My father felt the same way, which was why we rarely had fires in the fireplace at the old house. Every few years, though, he'd give in to pleas for a fire on Christmas Eve, setting the stage for disaster.

Dad had a good head for business, but anything even slightly mechanical left him befuddled and fuming. Asking him to adjust the fireplace draft would be like asking Ben Bernanke to fix a broken Weedeater. He'd begin by standing back and giving the fireplace a long, doleful look, as if inspecting for hairline cracks, or possibly demons. Then he'd yank furiously on the draft handle, trying in vain to distinguish "on" from "off." That done, he half-heartedly tried to start a fire.

Dad was a Presto Log man. Kindling was for sissies. His theory was that with help from rolled-up newspapers, Presto Logs would instantly produce a cheery, long-lasting blaze.

They didn't. The reality was anemic spluttering that wouldn't have warmed a closet. Combined with his damper adjustments, however, it was enough to fill the room with choking smoke that drove him to the edge of apoplexy. It drove my mother, who had spent the day baking Christmas treats and wanted everything to be perfect, to the edge of tears. That's when one of them invariably sounded the alarm:

"Call Howard!"

That would be Howard Snyder, the neighborhood fix-it man. Howard could fix anything. His shop and garage were all but held up by miscellaneous parts — beams, rafters, pipes, bolts, washers, springs, gaskets, every part imaginable in every vintage made. If you needed a speaker cone for a 1947 Philco radio or a ringer for a 1939 Bendix washer, Howard was your guy.

Howard didn't just fix things. He actually improved the original designs to make them work better, finishing the job with his signature expression of victory:

"That'll stop that foolishness."

Summoned for our fireplace emergencies, he'd tap here, prod there and, just like that, we had the Christmas Eve fire of our dreams.

Howard also averted real tragedy one morning by rescuing my father the day our coal furnace erupted. To this day, the vision of them bolting into my darkened bedroom from the furnace room, their frantic faces illuminated by buckets of flaming clinkers, is the closest I've come to a glimpse of hell.

Looking back, I should have watched more closely as Howard finessed finicky fireplaces, tamed beasts in the bowels of furnaces and fixed everything from slingshots to soapbox derby racers. I'd be a better man for it. I might even know how to stop the foolishness.

Now it's too late. Dad is gone, Howard is gone and I don't know a single fireplace trick.

I'm sorry about that, Valerie. But thanks for the memories.

'Maintenance Manor' Revisited
(May 9, 2010)

How long had it been since I peered into those rooms, so changed yet so familiar? After all the years, they still hadn't lost their power to overwhelm me.

When an old friend called to say that Maintenance Manor was for sale, I tried to ignore it. That old house had taken 13 years of my life. It was best forgotten.

Still, it was hard not to be curious. How much had it changed? Was it at long last finished? Maybe it was worth a peek, after all.

Maintenance Manor, for readers who missed my long-ago stories about it, was a North Boise fixer-upper. My wife and I bought it in the 1970s and spent years making it livable. It was the worst house in a nice neighborhood. With some work, we thought, it would be a good investment.

The best advice we got on that subject was my handyman father-in-law's. He was the first person we asked for a helping hand and a candid opinion of the place.

"If I were you, I'd knock it down and build a new house on the lot, " he said.

It's hard to fully explain that logic here, but a few details should give you an idea.

The house was then 70 years old. It had one bathroom, accessible only from a collapsing back porch. Wiring, plumbing — absolutely nothing met code. Leaky windows, zero insulation, a furnace that guzzled oil by the barrel. Sagging roof and floors, nightmare kitchen, basement dungeon. Everything about it was dismal, dilapidated, ugly.

So why did we buy it? The P Word. The myth that let the old house swallow the young couple: Potential.

We spent what should have been the best years of our lives chasing the P Word. We hired professionals to do the wiring, plumbing and furnace and did pretty much everything else ourselves. For years, and years, and years …

We knocked out walls and built new ones. The ceilings and the old walls that remained were in such bad shape that we had to sheetrock over them, a job that took forever. The woodwork was covered with gummy black paint that wouldn't strip off, sand off or burn off, so I had to make new woodwork for virtually the entire house.

We converted a tiny sewing room and absurdly large living room into a normal living room, a bathroom and two bedrooms. We installed new doors, windows, sinks, tubs, counters, cabinets, bookcases, lighting, flooring, siding, roofing… .

I was covered with wallboard mud one sunny afternoon when some friends pedaled by with tennis rackets. They waved. I wept.

When we were almost finished — are old houses ever truly finished? – we did an addition. A builder did the foundation, framing, wiring and plumbing; I did the rest. I was putting up the last piece of molding while the Realtor put up the pennants for the open house.

Even then, the job wasn't finished. The basement was still a dungeon, there still wasn't a garage and nagging projects still needed attention. We sold and never looked back.

Our timing, however, was vintage Woodward - just before the North End boom. Today, even with the price reduced, the asking price is almost four times what we got for it. Good timing beats sweat equity every time.

I did reap a lot of humor-in-adversity columns, though. Readers still comment on them. The columns and an education in the building trades were probably the best things about the whole experience.

Seeing the house again recently wasn't without some nice touches. Our daughters' small handprints and initials are still in the concrete I poured for the back porch. The addition still has my homemade woodwork. The front door I had so much trouble hanging is still hanging. And subsequent owners have done some needed modernizing.

The yard could use some work, though. There still isn't a garage and, well, as a real estate ad put it, it needs some work "to truly shine."

Next door, a once modest residence is hiding inside a sizable expansion and total makeover. Across the street, a humble home we remembered has vanished and a mansion has been built.

My father-in-law was just ahead of his time.

When the Last Kid Leaves Home
(Oct. 13, 2005)

It's almost spooky at our house these days. I woke up the other night and went downstairs to shut off a kitchen light that wasn't on. It was the moon, shining through the kitchen window. I thought it was our son, Mark, with a light on low for one of his nocturnal snacks.

I see him in his room, on the computer, around every other corner. I hear a television and think it's his voice. I start to reply, then realize he isn't home and won't be any time soon.

The youngest of three and our only boy, he left last week to attend school in another city. So, for the first time in over 30 years, there are no kids at our house. It's just the two of us now, rattling around in a house built for five — seven if you count a deceased dog and a bird that has long since flown. I haven't heard Slim the cockatiel whistling in the unaccustomed stillness yet, but then it's only been a couple of weeks.

Some of the changes have been all right. We buy a box of cereal and it's still there the next day. The stereo is getting a breather; the fury of Metallica is serenely absent. But these are small things. The big thing is more complicated.

When you first have kids, you feel like they'll be around forever. Then you make the mistake of blinking, and they're gone. That's when you start to wonder, in all that unaccustomed stillness, whether you wasted too much time along the way. You wonder whether you appreciated them enough, whether you did enough for them. Were you a good parent or not, and if you had it to do again what would you do differently?

Everyone who has kids knows the time will come to let go, but the generations don't seem to learn much about it from each other. A letter my parents wrote after I left for the Navy has come to mind a lot lately. They wrote about how quiet it was around the house — I was the last kid, too — and how they were struggling to fill the time once taken by parenting.

A few blinks later, I'm in exactly the same situation, never thought to ask them how they handled it, and now it's too late.

Should we do what they did — play golf, go fishing, buy an RV? Somehow I don't see myself in golf shoes and a pork-pie hat, muscling a gas hog around Arizona.

The problem is that we didn't plan for this. Like many baby boomers, we've been so wrapped up in work and being parents that we never gave a thought to how we'd fill the time when the parenting was over.

Canoeing, maybe? Canoes have always intrigued me; maybe we should buy a canoe.

No, that wouldn't work. My wife hates canoes.

Harleys?

No, too expensive.

Ballroom dancing?

No, one of us is way too clumsy.

One thing that does help fill the time is that we're having to do the things Mark used to do around the house, primarily cooking. He gets it from his grandfather, who also loved to cook.

We don't.

Maybe there's hope there. I have my eye on an Internet cookbook. Maybe a latent gene will kick in, and I'll while away my anecdotage puttering with pots and pans.

It's been an interesting couple of weeks. When people learn that the nest is newly empty, their reactions vary wildly. The wildest was an observation that with the kids gone we could walk around the house naked.

The neighborhood is breathless with anticipation.

The most insightful question anyone has asked so far is whether my wife and I still know how to talk to each other now that the kids are gone.

Yes. But a fair amount of the conversation tends to be about the kids.

Something that fills 30 years of your life doesn't just go away. You never really stop being a parent.

You do have to move on, though. It would be nice to tell you we have that part figured out, but we don't. Not yet, anyway. Talking about the kids and puttering in the kitchen will only get you so far, and continually seeing a face that isn't there is the worst kind of lonely.

If you have a suggestion, I'd love to hear it.

And if you read this, Mark, know that your parents still miss you like crazy.

When Summer Was Simple
(June 6, 2010)

Friday, as you know if you're a kid, parent or teacher, was the last day of school in Boise. So the question now is how the kids will keep from getting bored.

There are camps, of course. And summer classes and family trips and a numbing array of electronic pacifiers. But a lot of kids still get bored in the summer. One I know said she was actually dreading it.

When I was a kid — we won't get into how many geologic ages ago that was — that would have been unthinkable. I was reminded of this recently in a spate of emails from a childhood friend, Timmy Hally.

He goes by "Tim" now, of course, and lives in another state. But to me he'll always be Timmy Hally, the curly-haired kid who lived at 1311 N. 25th St. and had a dog named Queenie that bit me on the nose and three older brothers of whom I was moderately terrified.

His emails began in March, after the death of actor Fess Parker. Parker, you may recall, played Davy Crockett and later Daniel Boone in television series.

My friend Tim wanted to know if I ever had a Davy Crockett coonskin cap like the one he wore night and day until it fell apart.

The answer was that no serious ball player would be caught dead in a coonskin cap. Mine was a Cleveland Indians cap. I hadn't yet become a Chicago Cubs fan, but then as now had a gift for picking winners.

In the old neighborhood, boys' lives in the summertime revolved mainly around three things. One was baseball. We attended as many Boise Braves games as we could afford, listened to their away games on the radio and played baseball incessantly. Baseball to a lot of kids then was what computer games are to kids today.

"Remember our first coach in Little League?" Tim wrote. "He was an eighth-grader. No wonder we lost so much. Remember playing at Lowell Field?"

Remember? It was there that Flip Kleffner, a local boy who played briefly in the Big Leagues, practiced with us one day and hit the highest fly balls any of us had ever seen. One landed squarely on my nose, which had just recovered from Queenie. It was mortifying.

We could spend most of a morning oiling and shaping our mitts. The smell of the leather, the shades it turned as the color deepened, was almost hypnotic.

One of the other things around which life revolved was the municipal pool. We were there every day when it opened. Between doing cannonballs, working up the courage to go off of the high dive and flirting with the lifeguards, there wasn't time to be bored. (The lifeguards, who were older, considered us obnoxious pests.)

The third essential activity was actually a number of activities, loosely categorized as messing around. Tim remembered some I'd forgotten. Running through the sprinklers on a hot day, for example. Not like the pool, but still fun. And free.

"Remember melting crayons on your fence?" he wrote. "And playing marbles in the alley? And didn't we collect bottle caps?"

Yes. Bottle caps had cork liners then. If you took one out, pressed it against the inside of your shirt and pressed the cap against the outside and the liner, the cap stuck to the shirt. A poor kid's badge.

Can you imagine telling a bored kid today to go collect bottle caps?

Is it that they've become that much more sophisticated, or has a more sophisticated world lessened the capacity to appreciate simple pleasures?

Entertainment was never a problem in the world we knew. We roller-skated around the block, rode our bikes all over the North End, caught tadpoles, raced frogs, fished in the river, made soapbox derby racers.

The first rite of summer was the purchase of a new pair of U.S. Keds. No kid has ever looked forward to getting a Nintendo more than we did to getting new tennis shoes, which by summer's end would be in tatters.

I hope today's kids enjoy their electronics this summer. Really. But my wish for them is that they discover the joys of getting outdoors and creating their own fun. Summers of youth are too precious to waste on being bored.

Parents: Don't Blink
(June 3, 1993)

They should put warnings on babies.

"Caution. This kid is perishable. Blink and you'll miss it."

That way, new parents would know that what they were getting into was anything but permanent.

They would know the day was coming, and soon, when the kid would be grown and their jobs as parents would be all but over. They would know to make the most of the time while it lasted. They would know not to blink.

My daughter graduated from high school Tuesday night.

Can it be possible? It seems like yesterday that her mother was giving me the news of her existence. Now, more and more, we find ourselves talking about what our existence will be like without her.

It's a simple statement — my kid graduated from high school — but one that takes a while to accept. In fact, I'm still not convinced it's for real.

Her childhood didn't seem to pass quickly when it was happening. Now that it's gone, I feel like filing a complaint. I was cheated. No one warned me not to blink.

As we watched the graduates cross the stage to pick up their diplomas, I couldn't help recalling the day we turned her over to the system. It was a three-block walk to the neighborhood grade school. We each held a hand, ostensibly for her benefit.

Where had the pre-school years gone? When we were heating bottles and changing diapers and getting up in the night with bad dreams, it seemed as if that time would last forever. Who was this confident first-grader, arguing after one day of school that she knew the way and didn't need us anymore? She was genuinely miffed the day she caught me following along, just in case. It was a safe neighborhood, but you never knew when a kidnapper might be lurking behind a tree.

God, can that really be 12 years ago?

The smallest elementary school in town gave way to the biggest junior high school. We sat in the car for a long time her first morning there. The memory is as clear as if it had happened last week.

"I'm scared, Dad."

"Why?"

"It's so big."

I told her she'd get used to it in no time, but I was wrong. In no time, she was a sophomore.

High school was a blur. Sophomore orientation, driver's training, games, choir trips, final exams, graduation. When you're there, high school takes forever. When you have a kid there, it's a long heartbeat.

Now it's graduation, jobs, college. As the graduates flung their caps into the air, it was hard not to envy their youth, their elation, their innocence. They knew, but were still far from appreciating, that the cause of their joy was only a beginning.

What do you say to a kid starting out on that long journey? To be honest and work hard? To choose work that brings happiness as well as solvency? To practice safe sex and not forget to call home? To never forget that the people who held her hand on the first day of school will always be there, no matter how bad things get?

No, of course not. If they don't know by now … .

She stopped by the house to visit before rushing off to her senior party, a gesture her parents appreciated. Then she was gone for the night.

I fell asleep listening for the door that wouldn't be opening. The house was strangely, almost eerily, quiet.

Warning to new parents: Don't blink.

One of the Hardest Things a Father Does
(Aug. 25, 2003)

My daughter got married last Saturday. I did my best not to get involved.

It isn't that I didn't care; I just wanted to avoid the sort of stress that short-circuited parental synapses when my wife and I got married. To preserve his sanity amid the whirlwind of wedding planning, the father of the bride should be silent and, if possible, invisible.

The wisdom of this was confirmed when, in a weak moment, I suggested having the wedding in a park and the bride-to-be looked as if her father had a foot growing out of his chin. Her heart was set on a place that would cost nearly a week's pay to rent for a few hours.

"I just wanted to get married at the prettiest place I could find," she explained, near tears.

I shut my mouth, vowed to have no further opinions and wrote a check. Fathers of brides are nothing if not skilled check writers.

The strategy worked right up until the week of the wedding. My mouth remained shut, my blood pressure normal. There's something about the approach of a wedding, though, that makes the world spin in a different groove. Nerves fray; reason takes flight. Normally calm, sensible people suffer emotional meltdowns and lapses of sanity. Everyone wants so badly for things to go right that almost everything goes wrong.

A bridesmaid who had known about the wedding for a year decided at the last minute to fly off instead to exotic Chico, Calif. If not for a chance call on her cellphone as she was boarding her plane, she'd have shown up a week late.

Supposedly well-laid plans for the rehearsal dinner dissolved in a flurry of miscommunication and tears. And speaking of well-laid plans, our dog was due to have puppies precisely on the day of the wedding.

By the night before the big day, we had so many relatives sleeping at our house that they were bidding for floor space. I got up to read in the middle of the night and tripped over two cousins. We had some guy hanging around — usually at mealtimes — that no one had ever seen before. He left as suddenly as he came, probably in search of an asylum with a better menu.

I spent the morning of the big day painting cupboard doors. Don't ask me why; it seemed important at the time. It was going pretty well, too, until one of the younger relatives stepped in the paint and tracked it through the garage and down the front sidewalk. Moral: Don't even think about starting a project on your daughter's wedding day.

The wedding was at 6 p.m. By 4 p.m., almost everyone was decked out in formal attire and ready for the drive to the prettiest place the bride could find. By "almost," I mean everyone except the relatives who — after flying in from Seattle — abandoned all semblance of sanity, went shopping for a Harley and missed their ride to the ceremony they'd come 500 miles to see.

The ceremony itself, however, was just about perfect. The bride was tearfully radiant, the groom admirably composed. The puppies held off until it was over, and there wasn't even a hitch with the ring bearer — which I was counting on for comic relief. The groom is a K9 officer; the ring bearer was his dog.

They asked me to give a speech, which I got through almost without choking up at all.

I talked about the toddler whose sore paw her old man held when she was sick.

The little girl who curled up on his lap while he read her stories in an old rocking chair.

The 6-year-old whose hand he held the whole way to school on her first day in first grade, not because she needed it but because he did.

The young woman whose former boyfriend came back when she was diagnosed with cancer, stayed with her during the treatments that saved her life, and stayed on to become her husband.

I told him that giving away a daughter is one of the hardest things a father ever does. And I asked him to take good care of one of the most precious gifts I'd ever give anyone.

It turned out to be an absolutely beautiful wedding.

It's a funny thing, though. Now that it's over, the honeymooners are on a distant shore and the company is gone, I'd give a lot to have that old rocking chair back.

IDAHO ORIGINALS

History shows in the lines on the face of Dugout Dick, the last of Idaho's famed hermits. (Kim Hughes / Idaho Statesman)

My stock in trade for most of my Statesman career was writing stories about the people of my state — colorful characters that I came to call Idaho Originals.

Some were well known, others obscure.

Some were people I knew well, people I loved.

Some were strangers when I sought them out, but became friends for life.

All, in their own way, were unique. — Tim Woodward

The Halloween Grinch

(Nov. 3, 2005)

The most lavishly decorated house in my old neighborhood this Halloween had a cemetery in its front yard and a former owner spinning in his grave.

A neighbor who lives across the street called with the stunning news:

"You'll never guess which house is decorated to the hilt!" she said, giggling.

"Not Howard's!"

"Yes, Howard's! You wouldn't believe what the new owners have done!"

The new owners, Tom and Lisa Trutna, have a skeleton hanging from a tree, headstones in the yard, a giant spider crawling up a wall, skulls, fog, black lights...

What makes that funny for those who knew the late Howard Snyder is that he was the Halloween Grinch of North Boise. Howard despised Halloween in the way most people despise April 15 or the Monday after a vacation. It was odd, because in most other ways he was a wonderful man.

Howard was our neighborhood fix-it guy. His garage, basement and attic were filled to the rafters with nuts, bolts, wires, washers, welders, screws, brushes, solvents, springs, pipes, pulleys, tools and assorted parts. And he knew exactly where everything was. If you needed a camshaft for a '49 Packard, Howard could rummage around and have it for you in seconds.

He could fix anything, usually making it not only as good as new but better.

"That'll stop that foolishness," he'd invariably say after improving the design to correct a flaw.

He fixed our bikes, slingshots, model trains, soapbox derby racers. He taught us how to fish and hunt and fix things. He was a second father to virtually every kid in the neighborhood.

Except for one night of the year. On Halloween, he turned into a gun-wielding troll.

One of the many things Howard knew that no one else in the neighborhood knew was how to reload shotgun shells. He claimed to reload them with rock salt for burglars and trick or treaters, but I didn't believe him and found his attitude about Halloween patently annoying. One year, I decided to do something about it.

As always, his house was dark and silent on Halloween night. I watched it for a long time from the safety of my folks' back yard and, failing to see a single sign of life, worked up the nerve to go trick or treating there. It was getting late by then. Other kids, more sensible, had given the place a wide berth all evening. Shivering, I climbed the steps and put a clammy finger on the doorbell.

The result was shocking. Literally. One of the other things Howard knew about was electricity. His passion for Halloween trickery was so intense that he hot-wired his doorbell.

It wasn't a bad shock, but it was rude enough that I decided to go for broke and soap his windows. I was reaching for the living-room picture window with my bar of soap when a familiar voice stopped me.

"Don't touch that window!"

I wheeled around and, silhouetted in the crook of a tree behind me, was a man brandishing a shotgun.

No one in the history of Halloween has run faster.

He didn't shoot, of course. To the best of my knowledge, he never shot at anything that wasn't in season. The shotgun probably wasn't even loaded.

Howard passed away a few years ago at age 96. People who didn't know him talk about what a grump he supposedly was, but I knew him well and never knew him to be anything but a friend and mentor.

Except on Halloween. Long after the treats of this and other Halloweens are gone and forgotten, I'll still remember the heart-pounding excitement of almost soaping his windows. Just the memory of the silhouette in the crook of the tree gives me the chills in a way no horror movie has before or since.

I think Howard the Halloween Grinch was a throwback to a more innocent time, when Halloween included as many tricks as it did treats, and chocolate was a distant second to goose bumps.

Big Shot
(Nov. 16, 2008)

Many Idahoans who knew Paul B. Larsen knew him as a Realtor. Newspapers spell that word with an upper-case "R" because it's a trademark, but I'd do it in his case even if it weren't. He was an upper-case guy.

Larsen, who died Oct. 27 at 99, was a prominent Boise businessmen when I was growing up here. His name was on radio, TV, signboards. He was an officer in important organizations, a member of the exclusive Arid Club and was said to have sold more hotels and motels than any real estate broker in the country. He played golf with J.R. Simplot.

This was the formidable, no-nonsense businessman my father propositioned with what must have struck him as one of the most wild-eyed schemes ever to cross his desk.

The originator of the scheme was a teen-aged me. My life then was playing in a rock group, and we'd just been fired from our one regular gig in Boise for starting late. We'd driven halfway across Oregon in a blizzard to get there and were only half an hour late — which we thought was almost heroic — but there was no arguing. Our best job was gone.

I was moping around thinking the world had ended when an idea struck. It was bold. It was genius. It was perfect.

We would re-open the Fiesta. A second-floor ballroom at 6th and Idaho, the Fiesta had been the most popular dance hall in town until its closure a couple of years earlier. It was an old Arthur Murray Dance Studio, run as a teenage ballroom by a businessman named Mel Day.

The next evening found me in Day's living room, pleading with him to reopen.

Judging by level of his enthusiasm, you'd have thought I'd suggested a fun bus to Idaho Falls. He made it clear that there was no way in heaven or hell he was getting back into the dance business.

"But you might talk to Paul Larsen," he said. "He owns the building."

Paul Larsen? The real estate magnate? A big shot like him leasing to some scruffy rock group? Right.

It took several days to work up the nerve to call him. It was pretty much a one-way conversation, mostly involving stammering on my part, but it ended with a scintilla of hope.

"Ask your Dad if he'll sign the lease," he said. "If he will, make an appointment to see me."

Persuading Dad took some doing. He, after all, was the one who'd be liable if we failed to pay the rent, or some drunk got thrown through a window (this happened), or worse.

On the other hand, Dad was a businessman himself. I think he half-heartedly hoped it would launch me on a business career. Whatever his hopes, we met with Larsen, who couldn't have been nicer. The lease was signed; life was good again.

Dad's role ended with his signature, so we really were about to get an education in running a small business. It was up to us to sponsor and advertise the dances. We had to pay bills, hire cashiers, cops, a bouncer, clean-up crew and people to sell soft drinks. Not to mention endlessly practicing to have new songs ready every Saturday night. It was a big commitment for a bunch of high-school kids.

Life eventually teaches us that dreams seldom come true, and often only partially when they do. But this one exceeded all expectations. On opening night, the place was jammed. We paid the bills for the month and had money left over, a happy circumstance that lasted until weddings and draft notices ended the ride 18 months later.

It was the most money any of us had ever seen. We had dresser drawers crammed with it. But the money was secondary. For a band, nothing is like playing for a big, enthusiastic crowd on a night when the group is really clicking, which is why some of us are still doing it all these years later.

One of the more unusual memories from those days is of a distinguished-looking man standing near the back of the ballroom. He seemed ancient compared with the dancers around him, but then he would only have been in his late 50s. My guess at the time was that Larsen had come to see whether his faith in us was justified. I prayed that no one would give our mercurial bouncer an excuse to throw someone through a window, but nothing bad happened. The man just stood there, saying nothing, wearing an enigmatic smile. Then he was gone.

Only after his death did I learn that as a young man he played in "Paul's Dance Band."

"It was a big band," his son-in-law, Ron Thurber, said. "They traveled clear up into Canada."

That would explain his surprising readiness to lease a valuable Downtown building to a bunch of kids. Maybe in us he saw himself in his youth.

I never saw him again, which is a shame because his faith in the boys we were led to one of the best times of my life. If it were possible to defy death and get a message to him, it would be simple and heartfelt: Thanks for saying yes.

Farewell to the Road
(Feb. 15, 1981)

Bert Woodward (Provided by Tim Woodward)

As near as he can recall, Bert Woodward first slid behind the wheel of an automobile in 1918, when he was 16 years old. It was a Dodge. He and some other boys rented it from the local garage in their hometown of Cripple Creek, Colo., and took turns driving the 125 miles to Denver. It took about four hours.

"Until that trip, I don't think I'd ever driven before," he said. "There weren't any paved roads in those days, of course, so it took a lot longer to go anywhere."

I asked if the boys had had to take driving lessons in order to rent the car.

"No, there wasn't any such thing as driving lessons," he replied. "You didn't need a license, either. You just started it up and took off."

Times change. Last month, on the occasion of his 79th birthday, the state refused to renew his driver's license. The doctor and the officials agreed: His eyesight wasn't good enough.

I am not writing this because Bert Woodward is my father or because anyone is angry about what happened or thinks it was unfair. Even he admits that it was the right decision. But as he surrenders his license after more than 60 years on the public highways, it seems clear that an era is ending. His history parallels that of the automobile, and there aren't many people left who can say that.

His first car was a 1923 Model T, the automobile E.B. White lovingly recalled in an essay titled Farewell My Lovely:

"It was the miracle God had wrought. And it was patently the sort of thing that could only happen once. Mechanically uncanny, it was like nothing that had ever come to the world before."

My father bought his Model T new. It cost $600. He was 21 and had just been hired as the Fuller Brush Company's man in Laramie, Wyo. He and the Ford covered the Wyoming territory together, and the thought of it still makes him smile.

"The radiator used to boil all the time, especially in the mountains, and you'd have to carry a bucket to get water from the creek when it heated up … If you forgot to set the spark advance, it'd kick like the dickens when you cranked it. For those days, it was a sporty car, though – a lot better than the one I traded it in on."

He drove it two years and traded it on a Durant Star Coupe.

"Durant was supposed to be the most revolutionary car maker in the world," he said. "They said the Star Coupe would revolutionize the automotive industry. It had aluminum pistons, which made it real snappy to drive, but it didn't hold up. In just a few months I was putting more oil in it than gas, so I got rid of it. I put in the heaviest oil I could find and traded it on a Chevrolet."

Dad probably didn't realize it at the time, but the job in Wyoming was the beginning of a 58-year career as a salesman. My father never cheated anyone or made a dishonest or unethical sale in his life. I once saw him find a nickel on the floor of a supermarket and turn it in as lost property. Scores of his customers became lifelong friends. He can't cross the street without running into one of them.

In 1929 he got a job selling for the Procter & Gamble Co. The company supplied its salesmen's cars, and he figures he drove them an average of 30,000 miles a year for seven years. In his lifetime, he drove something like a million miles, enough to go around the world more than 400 times.

The Model T, the Star Coupe and the Chevrolet were followed in turn by a 1936 Oldsmobile, a 1940 Oldsmobile, a 1940 Buick, and a 1936 Studebaker, the car he had when I was born. The first of his cars that I remember was a 1947 Buick. It was blue and had felt upholstery – except for the armrests, which were covered with mohair. My mother used to say that my butch haircut felt just like the mohair armrests in the Buick.

The Buick took my father to the Northwest grocers who purchased his lines of food products. It must have been a good car because in 1955 he bought another Buick. He and my mother rode the train to the factory in Flint, Mich., and drove the new job back to Idaho. I had been lobbying for a used Oldsmobile with a big red light on the dashboard, but when I saw the new Buick it was love at first sight. It was a Buick Special, Nile Green with a white top. Dad said he could steer it with one finger. He drove it for 12 years and more than 100,000 miles. At trade-in time he was selling lawn sprinkling systems for his own company.

A car is a mystifying thing – an assembly of lifeless objects to which its owner, in utter defiance of the laws of biology and physics, somehow imparts the gift of life. Cars are universally seen as having human traits. The inanimate parts collection is described as being loyal, trustworthy, heroic, temperamental, obstinate, even sneaky. If a car turns on you, you hate it as surely as you would a bitter foe. Conversely, the car that proves itself "loyal" becomes an object of wistful affection.

Dad hated to sell the Buick. He even talked of keeping it as a fishing car. I don't remember the last time he went fishing.

The Buick was followed by two Pontiacs and a Volvo, his first foreign car and the last he will own. A dozen cars in six decades. I asked which were his favorites.

"The '36 Oldsmobile was a good car," he said. "And the '55 Buick was one of my favorites, and this one, the Volvo … After all those years of driving, I hate to give it up. It's about like losing your right arm."

Marguerite O'Leary Woodward: 1913-2005
(Dec. 8, 2005)

Marguerite O'Leary Woodward (Provided by Tim Woodward)

When I remember my mother, who died the day before Thanksgiving, I won't think of a 92-year-old woman clinging to life. I'll remember a younger woman, laughing.

She was one of those people who unfailingly sees humor in adversity. When her 1952 Nash Rambler overheated on a family trip to Yellowstone, she stood in the middle of the highway and laughed. We were stuck in a broiling desert with no water and her car doing a highly successful imitation of Old Faithful, and she thought it was hysterical.

That was my mother for you. She could turn oral surgery into a good time.

Born Marguerite O'Leary in Walla Walla, Wash., she grew up in Boise and came of age during the Depression. She was selling hosiery at the now-defunct Falk's Department Store downtown when my father came in to buy some as a gift for his mother, and so began a courtship. The two of them couldn't have been more different — he with his inherited British reserve and she with her Irish spontaneity. But their marriage lasted until his death in 1985.

She was fond of saying that she was "as Irish as Paddy's pig." We never knew who Paddy was, let alone his pig, but there it was. She had a saying for virtually any situation:

"This isn't worth a hill of beans."

"She made me feel like 2 cents waiting for change."

"You get used to hanging if you hang long enough."

Smart and perceptive, she also could be wildly illogical. Told while she and Dad were planning a once-in-a-lifetime trip to Europe that the standard form of greeting in Germany was "guten tag (good day)," she was incensed:

"Guten tag! Why don't they just say 'hello?' If 'hello' is what they mean, why not say it and be done with it? Why beat around the bush with this 'guten tag' business?"

Her unorthodox style of reasoning could be disarming. She loved sporty cars and drove the way she did everything else — no beating around the bush. The last car she owned was a royal blue Honda two-seater with personalized plates "BLU BABY." Most of the cops in town knew it.

"I wasn't the one who was speeding," she'd tell them. "It's this car of mine, officer. This little blue baby just wants to get out and go."

It worked every time. She never once got a ticket.

In all the years, we had just one serious argument. I was a teenager, played in a band and had grown my hair long, though modestly so by today's standards. She hated it, and it reached the point that we stopped speaking. When she did speak, it was to issue an ultimatum:

"From now on, you're doing your own cooking and your own laundry until you get that hair cut!"

"Fine!" I snapped back.

Later, she knocked softly on my door, came in and asked why a boy brought up on crew cuts would suddenly want long hair. I replied that it was the style and I liked it.

"Oh," she said, sounding surprised. Relieved that it wasn't something subversive — fear of Communist plots ran deep at our house — she resumed her cheerful demeanor and never mentioned the hair issue again. Plots, Communist or otherwise, were alien and frightening. Style she appreciated.

She taught me to tie my shoes and say my prayers, to honor my elders, value my friends, always tell the truth, not take anything that wasn't mine and to love America, work hard and never lose my sense of humor or give up.

"You have to have stick-to-it-iveness," she told me a zillion times. "Nobody likes a quitter."

One of the best things she passed on to me was her love of music. My father was a wonderful man, but he couldn't have carried a tune in a Hummer. Mom was forever singing, humming, listening to the radio. One day she interrupted me in the middle of a song I was playing on the stereo.

"Is that the Beatles?" she asked.

"Yes."

"Really? Their voices sound beautiful together. Let's listen to it again."

64

We did, several times. She wasn't trying to butter me up or anything; she honestly liked the song. It was one of our best moments together. All the other guys' moms hated the Beatles.

When I was 16, she secretly paid the balance on a guitar I'd been saving for and had it waiting on Christmas morning. It was the best present I ever received, or ever will.

Never a patient woman, she told me several times during the last year of her life that she'd lived long enough, or, as she put it, "I just want to go home."

She was tired of beating around the final bush, ready to see what was on the other side. Knowing that helped when it actually happened.

It took a couple of days, though, for the obvious to sink in — that for the first time in my life I have no parents. Not even Mom had a saying for the way that makes you feel.

On the good side, the suffering of her old age is over. She got her wish and went home.

Sometimes, when no one's around and the house is quiet, I can almost hear her laughing.

Poore is Rich
(Jan. 3, 1988)

The call came at noon Christmas.

Long-distance calls from the boss almost never mean good news, but this was almost incomprehensible.

A stroke?

Jim Poore?

The words didn't fit. Jim Poore — the rock of The Statesman's sports staff, the guy who could hit a softball out of the galaxy and thought nothing of driving all night after working all day on a distant game, a man whose love of life was as big as his size 52 suits — had had a stroke?

Come on, boss.

I'll never forget the day I met him. He was laying claim to his half of the elevator at the old Statesman building when he spotted the new rookie, hired the day before as the Canyon County reporter, and in typical Poore fashion shouted across the lobby.

"Hey, Woodward! Get on and we'll ride up together."

One of the things I was to learn in the years ahead was that these words, or variations of them, would take us far beyond the lobby of 300 N. 6th St.

"Who are you?" I asked. "And how did you know my name?"

"Jim Poore," he said. "We had a journalism class together. You went the first day and never came back."

I'd almost forgotten. Six years earlier, I had dropped a reporting class at Boise Junior College. Jim hadn't forgotten, though. He never forgot anyone.

"Hey, Woodward!" he'd shout across the newsroom. "Remember Joe Smith?"

"Who?"

"Joe Smith. His paper just won the Pulitzer Prize."

"Who's Joe Smith?"

"You remember. An intern here 10 or 12 years ago. Black hair. He wore bow ties and drove an old Ford and was always spilling cigarette ashes on everything."

I couldn't remember the man's name; Jim remembered his clothes, his car, his cigarettes. And on the very same day, he might have forgotten to turn off his stove, make an overdue payment or keep an appointment with the IRS.

He once went three years without filing a tax return. Anyone else would have been flogged, but Jim left the agents laughing, and got money back.

He was a successful man on the razor of financial chaos. Lost paychecks turned up in obscure drawers or under car seats. Instead of keeping a record of his checks, he wrote them until the overdrafts arrived, then stopped writing them for a while. Fines and late fees were routine.

"Hey, Woodward!" he said one afternoon (on deadline). "Come with me to the library. I have to pay a fine."

So how much can a library fine be?

"That will be $106," an unsmiling librarian said.

It was a golden moment, even for Jim.

To his friends, there was a simple explanation. He didn't care about practical things. He cared about people.

"Hey, Woodward!" he said one day in 1977. "I've got this great idea for a book we could write, but it's set in Russia and to do it right we'd have to go there."

"What! I can't afford to go to Russia."

"That's OK. I'll pay your way."

And he did. I paid back half and promised the rest, but he wouldn't hear of it. Doing things for his friends was one of his greatest pleasures.

If a man's worth can be measured in friends, he may have been the richest man in Idaho. In just a few days, he broke the hospital's all-time record for numbers of visitors. Some of the sports world's greatest legends sent messages saying he was in their prayers.

It seems strange to be writing about him in the past tense, as if he were gone instead of just in a coma.

He'll be back, of course. Without Jim Poore, The Statesman wouldn't be The Statesman.

Why, just the other day he was talking about this great idea he had for a story.

"Hey, Woodward!" he said. "I've got an incredible idea for a series we could do. It's a jungle cruise …"

There's never been a story I wanted more.

Remembering Romaine
(Jan. 1, 2007)

In my most vivid memory of former Statesman columnist Romaine Galey Hon, who died Dec. 23, she's pushing a mansion down Warm Springs Avenue.

The mansion was the historic Bishop's House, which she'd spent years working to save from the wrecking ball and move to its current location by the old penitentiary. When moving day came and the gargantuan truck carrying the turreted mansion stalled at a stoplight, she actually got behind it and pushed.

That was Romaine. A woman of action — regardless of the odds or what anyone thought. If a thing was worth doing, it was worth going all out.

Statesman readers knew her as the longtime author of a column on food and cooking. She traveled the world at her own expense, collecting recipes and friends wherever she went. One column might feature an exotic recipe from France, the next a trade secret from a New York chef, the next the recipe for your favorite soup at a local diner. Her columns on recreating the cinnamon rolls served at a long-closed Boise eatery are among the best-read things the Statesman has ever published.

A former editor learned the extent of her popularity after dropping her column in 2003 as part of a round of budget-cutting. It was an unpopular decision, as evidenced by a deluge of protest letters, but no one missed the column more than its author. I held her sore paw more than once over it. As happens with all columnists who stick with it long enough, the column had become part of her identity.

But only a part. Without being flamboyant or seeking attention, Romaine was one of our bona fide local characters. A divorcee, she lived alone in an imposing red-brick and gingerbread mansion on Main Street just short of Warm Springs Avenue. Her parents had once owned it and the house next door, where she was raised. Its upper floors had been converted to apartments, which she rented to people who needed a place to live more than she needed the money.

"The only word I can think of to describe her is Bohemian, but she was more than that," former renter Bobbie Cunningham said. "When I was young and new to Boise, my husband and I lived in a beautiful upstairs apartment in her house. Our rent was only $100 a month, but we had to vacuum the stairs and rake the leaves as part of the deal.

"... She had people living there who couldn't afford to live anywhere else. One was mentally ill. She took people in that no one else would. She got them jobs and made sure they were OK. And downstairs in her beautiful home, which was like walking into a Charles Dickens story, she'd be having fundraisers for the Democratic Party."

Her parties were legendary for their oddness. Cunningham remembers her keeping bottles that had once contained expensive wine and filling them with Yosemite Road, which sold for a few bucks a gallon. People thought she was joking when she invited them to her "VD Party," until the lights went down and she began showing slides of people ravaged by venereal disease.

"You need to know what can happen," she told her startled audience. "You need to be careful."

It was a somber group that filed out her door that night, wondering at the reasoning that had inspired the guest list.

Her social circle included everyone from struggling artists to the rich and powerful. I didn't know how rich and powerful until 1989, the year the Chicago Cubs played the San Francisco Giants for the National League Pennant. Romaine had often said that if my star-crossed Cubs ever made it to the playoffs a Chicago friend of hers could get me tickets, so I decided to call her bluff. A few days later, she called back.

"Meet my friend Tuesday morning at the Drake Hotel," she said.

When I offered to pay her for the tickets, Romaine's elegant-looking friend at the equally elegant hotel looked at me as if I had a foot growing out of my forehead. Only after returning home did I learn that her husband was the president of the Chicago Tribune Co., which owns the Cubs. Romaine hadn't thought it was worth mentioning.

She was such a paradox. She was equally at home dining in a fine Paris restaurant or at the humble State Court Cafe, which we did the week it closed. She was on a first-name basis with members of the Arid Club set and with penniless students. She lived in a mansion, but not long before her death wrote a letter to a senior forum saying she'd qualify for financial aid but for her "meager savings."

Much of her life is and will probably always be a mystery to me. But mine is richer for having shared part of it.

Just before Thanksgiving, she e-mailed to say her doctor had found a tumor.

"I am fine about my future, whether it be long or short," she wrote.

It was shorter than anyone knew. We made plans to meet for a drink during the holidays, never dreaming that that would be too late. So today, while everyone else is ringing in the New Year, I'm going to slip away to a quiet spot, pour a shot of cheap wine into the most expensive glass I can find, and drink a lonesome toast to my departed friend.

The Stinker
(April 24, 1994)

If you've passed the corner of Franklin and Maple Grove roads lately, you've seen the signs identifying the site of the future Farris Lind Boy Scout Center. But do you know who Farris Lind was?

If not, you missed something.

He was a legend. If you're new to the state, or even if you aren't, you can't help learning from his story.

Lind was known as a wealthy and fiercely independent businessman, the founder of the Fearless Farris Stinker service stations. But his story began in poverty, on a farm near Twin Falls.

He had one pair of pants. He and his brother shared an unheated room, little more than a lean-to attached to their farmhouse. Kids from town called it a shack.

Instead of wearing him down, poverty made him determined. He vowed to escape a life of "stoop labor" in the fields. And escape he did.

Lind was fascinated by airplanes. He didn't have money for college, but he saved enough for training that allowed him to soar above the fields in a crop-duster. That's how he got the name "Fearless Farris," by working the farms with the tightest, most dangerous turns.

In 1940, he borrowed $5 for a trip to Boise to see Gov. Chase Clark, who had been critical of Idaho's high gasoline prices. Then 25, Lind spent the night in his car, shaved in a gas station. He had never met Clark and didn't have an appointment, but he left that day with a lease to open a cut-rate service station on state land at 17th and Front.

By the mid-'70s, Lind was selling more gas than anyone in Idaho. The business that began with a $25-a-month lease was selling $30 million a year in five states.

Much of it was due to its owner's sense of humor. The company logo was a skunk with boxing gloves, a "Stinker" fighting Big Oil. The thing that endeared the Stinker to customers, however, was a series of signs along desolate stretches of desert highways:

"If you lived here, you'd be home now."

"Mashed Cat, Idaho."

"Running rabbits have right of way."

A sign overlooking an outcropping of round rocks near Bliss advertised "Petrified watermelons. Take some home to your mother-in-law."

A sign on a simmering stretch of desert, miles from a lake or even a puddle, warned passersby that there was "No fishing within 100 yards."

Poking fun at himself, Lind advised motorists that "the only corn raised in this desert are these signs."

The signs were taken down in the '60s, victims of the Highway Beautification Act. It was a sad time for countless travelers, who had come to rely on them for a smile and a break in the monotony.

Sadder still was the day in 1963 when the Stinker was vaccinated for polio. A violent headache followed. Four days after that, he was in an iron lung.

Lind didn't let polio stop him. He kept his sense of humor, continued to run his business, traveled in a specially equipped motor home.

"The key was to pretend there was nothing wrong with me," he once said. "I should endeavor to act normal, ignore pain and conduct business as usual."

This from a man paralyzed from the neck down.

The Farris Lind story — something to keep in mind when tempted to snivel over ordinary problems.

Don Dick, Institution
(March 1, 2000)

If you didn't know Don Dick, whose funeral was Tuesday after he lost his long battle with cancer last week, you're probably a newcomer to Boise. Don was an Old Boise guy, and I mean that in the best possible way.

He spent 30 years in the gardening business, but it seemed longer. He was one of those people who early in life acquire the status of local institutions. Part of it was his knowledge, which made him indispensable to the brown-thumb crowd, but a larger part of it was the man himself. Don was a big, strapping fellow with a friendly, open face and a smile as bright and welcoming as the flowers he loved. To know him five minutes was to like him for life.

Before there was a mall or a Connector or a Pavilion, Don Dick was a household word. Boise was a smaller town then, with limited entertainment options. On weekends, people flocked to the Union Farm & Garden Store, where he spent most of his working years. He once said that everyone in town had been there at one time or another, not to buy things but to see Amos and Sarge, the store's talking parrots.

It's hard to remember a time when he wasn't part of the public consciousness. He had a gardening show on the radio, appeared on television, and, if he'd wanted, could have been elected mayor. When I met him in person for the first time, it was like meeting an old friend. My wife and I had just bought an old house with a problem-ridden yard and desperately needed help. Luckily, Don and the store he managed were just a few blocks away.

It probably isn't overstating it by much to say that he put a tree, a bush or an idea in about every yard in town. He sold me the oddments needed for three yards — trees, shrubs, grass seed, fertilizer, hoses, annuals, perennials, herbicides, pesticides, sprays, sprayers. He sold me a lawnmower that ran without complaint for 25 summers and was still running when I traded it for a newer, less-reliable model. But it wasn't what he sold that people valued most. His advice, usually given free, was priceless.

If a problem couldn't be diagnosed in the store, he happily made house calls. I don't know how many times he drove to my home to pull up a tuft of dying grass or eyeball a sickly tree and make an on-the-spot analysis. In his later years, with the store closed and the medical bills piling up, he had to charge a modest fee for his house calls. I never heard of anyone complaining.

His advice is ever in mind at puttering time:

"Put your roses to bed wet."

The words return every fall as I put the hoses away for the winter, then drag them out again for a final watering.

"Watch as much football as you can stand on Thanksgiving, then go out and fertilize your lawn."

I do, to the amusement of neighbors who consider me the halftime show.

"Treat crabgrass when the forsythia are blooming."

If crabgrass had flowers, he probably would have liked it. He often said his favorite flower was whatever was blooming.

So many people revered his advice — and his memory — that they braved a cold rain Tuesday to fill St. Mark's Church for his funeral and the Basque Center for a memorial lunch.

Later, I drove by the old store where he once held court amid a cacophony of chattering parrots. It was silent, dark, dreary. The man who gave it life was gone, nothing was blooming, and spring seemed far away.

Zamzow's Garden
(June 10, 2008)

Bernie Zamzow, in his beloved garden. (Chris Butler / Idaho Statesman)

In a green oasis behind the Fairview Avenue Zamzows store, a vigorous man of 92 works in his garden — as he has nearly every summer for 68 years.

His parents, August and Carmalita Zamzow, opened the store, the original Zamzows, in 1933. Bernie Zamzow and his late wife, Helen, built their home on a half acre behind it in 1940. The woman who sold them the land wanted him to buy 10 acres. It was $400 an acre, though, and he didn't want to go into debt.

"I can still hear her saying, 'Young man, you'll be sorry!'" he said. "I know of an acre near here that sold not too long ago for $180,000, but I was never sorry. I have everything I need here."

Most customers who shop at the store have no idea that a picture-perfect garden is tucked away behind it. Zamzow returns from his winter home in Arizona when the soil is warm enough to work — he's been known to bring plant starts home with him in a suitcase — and spends virtually every day tending his garden, eschewing power equipment for hand tools and the exotic for the tried and true.

"I've tried some of those fancy tomatoes, but I don't like them," he said during a break in one of his daily hoeing sessions. "I plant the Early Girls and others I like. If you don't like it, why plant it?"

Manicured rows of vegetables fill a space behind and larger than his back lawn. Lettuce, tomatoes, carrots, radishes, beets and other irrigated crops all but spring from the soil. Berry bushes and fruit trees line the yard.

A fence separates the yard from what he calls "the back 40," land that belongs to his neighbors but he uses to grow a second garden: corn, squash, beans, rhubarb, sweet potatoes, melons. He figures he gives away about 90 percent of what he grows.

"If I don't have anybody who wants it, I take it over to the store," he said. "There's always a customer who'll take it."

His tips for growing a successful garden: Add compost every year and balance it with organic fertilizer. Irrigate rather than sprinkling. Keep insects at bay with a mixture of vinegar and water.

"And a hoe doesn't hurt."

Lean and tan in jeans, a T-shirt and a Zamzows ball cap, he looks younger than his years. When it's too wet to work in the garden, he trims bushes or trees or works around the house. At 92, he thinks nothing of climbing onto the roof to fix a shingle or scaling a tree trunk to saw off a limb.

"Guys have asked to mow the lawn, and I tell them if they did it, what would I have to do? I don't need anybody to do my work for me."

His work gloves are so worn they have holes in the knuckles.

Charlotte Eller, a friend, says he "owes his longevity to exercise. He rides his bike everywhere. He still goes dancing. He works hard, and he plays hard."

Playing hard would include gold, silver and bronze horseshoe-pitching medals in the Senior Olympics.

Jim Zamzow, who, with his brother Rick owns and operates 10 Zamzows stores, credits his father with saving the family business: "We make a big fuss about grandmother and grandfather and what we're doing now, but the one who held it all together was Dad. Without him, we wouldn't have the business. It was failing when he came back from World War II. He salvaged it with hard work and the business experience he got as an Army supply officer."

Even in the Army, he had a garden. One of Jim Zamzow's favorite stories is of his father "sitting in a chair with a shotgun, waiting for a gopher that was eating his carrots. He waited all day. When the carrots started wiggling, he started blasting."

Moral: Don't get between a gardener and his vegetables.

"I guess I'm just a farmer at heart," he said. "Gardening is fun for me. I like to grow things, and I like fruits and vegetables.

"To me it's invigorating to plant things and see them come up, grow, mature and produce edible food. I never get tired of it."

A Brick for Gary Hughes
(Oct. 5, 1986)

It was, as Boise Redevelopment Agency co-Chairman Ron Twilegar put it, "a wonderful day for Boise." After 22 years, the redevelopment agency was building something instead of tearing it down.

The mood of the ground-breaking last week for downtown's public plaza could not have been more festive, or upbeat. A band played, cheerleaders cheered, and balloons filled the air as the mayor turned over the first bit of earth. Even the weather cooperated, providing one of the few sunny days of the Arctic Indian summer.

It was a day for compliments. Speaker after speaker made certain that no one had been overlooked, from the Highway District to the congressional delegation. The mayor, who went so far as to work in a positive comment about a trailer convention, spoke in especially radiant terms of his fellow dignitaries, who sat somberly on the stage, as if there were nothing the least bit amusing about the combination of three-piece suits and hard hats.

A moment of inspired irony came when the mayor asked the whereabouts of the man who was supposed to have been stationed at the controls of the backhoe, but had disappeared. Twenty-two years of waiting, and he wasn't ready.

Twenty-two years generally is accepted as the amount of time the city has spent on its redevelopment program. A conflicting view, however, was provided by Robert Mather, chairman of the Boise Auditorium District. As Mather put it, the elapsed time was only two years, the amount of time "the new B.R.A." has been in existence.

"I think that's something we can all be proud of," he enthusiastically told the crowd.

The remark was punctuated by a pause for applause that never came, and the awkward silence seemed a fitting time to reflect on all the years and all the people it really had taken to reach what was modestly hailed as downtown's "new beginning."

Where, for example, was Dick Eardley, the mayor who devoted a good part of his life to the redevelopment dream? Or Jay Amyx, his predecessor, who was equally committed to the downtown will-o'-the-wisp?

Where were Carroll Sellars and Chuck Newhouse and Don Day? Or Ralph McAdams or Fred Kopke or Marge Ewing, or any other of the redevelopment veterans who poured their years and their talents into the dream? Had anyone thought to invite them?

Most of all, I couldn't help wondering whether anyone had thought – for even a brief moment of the new beginning – about Gary Hughes.

A block from where the dignitaries were congratulating one another on the impending construction of the plaza, a frail little man named Gary Hughes once gave a similarly upbeat speech during a similarly festive ceremony. The year was 1973. The occasion was the impending construction of the One Capital Center building, which, if memory serves, also was considered a new beginning.

One Capital Center was among the successful projects in which the redevelopment agency has been involved, and for which it seldom receives credit. Others include the Statehouse Inn, the Front Street parking garage and the Idaho First National Bank tower, now reduced to insignificance in the euphoria of Mather's time machine and the new B.R.A.'s personalized bricks.

As executive director of the B.R.A. for the last five years of his life, Hughes was intimately involved in its projects, successful and otherwise. If there had been a few more successes, he might be alive today.

He was the most nervous man I ever knew. The impossible goal of building a downtown regional shopping center he considered his personal responsibility, and it made of him a driven and haunted man. His voice shook; his hands trembled. He fidgeted so much and so violently that it took an effort not to shake or slap him to his senses, before his molecules began to come apart.

When I was a reporter on the redevelopment beat, he frequently called me at home to ask what I'd written, or was thinking of writing, about his beloved agency. If the news was bad, as it often was, he'd plead with me not to use it. He knew it was useless, but he never stopped trying. He so desperately wanted the agency's efforts to be perceived as successful that it was hard to know whether he realized it when they weren't.

It never was established whether he killed himself because of downtown, but it was widely suspected. They found him on his patio, with a shotgun at his side and a hole in his chest.

I think he would have enjoyed last week's new beginning, despite its almost total disregard for those who made the beginnings that led to it.

And if it isn't too much to ask, I think that when the plaza is finished, it should include a small remembrance of the man who cared so deeply about the downtown dream: a brick for Gary Hughes.

Bookworm
(Dec. 5, 2010)

Boise State University Professor Tom Trusky lived in a North Boise house that needed paint and insulation, didn't meet electrical codes and had bricks missing from a chimney. He lived so frugally that the gift in his will stunned even his closest friends.

Brilliant but eccentric, Trusky didn't learn to drive or own a car until he was middle-aged. Having finally bought one, he went 35,000 miles between oil changes.

His favored mode of transportation: a battered Peugeot bicycle. Boise State's lowest paid English teacher for years, he waited until late in his life — and then only as a long-distance necessity — to buy a telephone.

"He wasn't a monk, but he lived like one," his friend and former student Troy Passey said.

Trusky, who died a year ago of heart failure at 65, worked out of a home office with a puny baseboard heater and an office at Boise State rampant with clutter.

"I thought he was disorganized, but that was because I saw his office with piles of stuff everywhere," said Cort Conley, another friend. "But the more I looked through his papers after he died, the more stunned I was."

Trusky, the seemingly disorganized professor, had filed everything from postcards to art books. The most valuable he had banked.

"There were books I know he paid over $500 for 10 years ago on a teacher's salary," Conley said. "Books, poems, letters — everything was in acid-proof folders, coded and alphabetized. He saved anything he thought might have literary merit, and it was already archived."

But it was the contents of his U.S. Bank safe-deposit box that left Trusky associates reeling. Named as his personal representative in his will, Conley was staggered to open the box and find a dozen books by acclaimed artist-bookmaker James Castle.

Trusky was Castle's biographer; Castle was one of Trusky's many obsessions. But no one knew the extent or value of the Castle collection he'd locked away and left to Boise State in his will.

"I knew he had some of Castle's work, but when I went through it, I was blown away by how many drawings he had," Passey said. "I don't think you can buy a Castle drawing today for less than $5,000."

Greg Kucera, who sells Castle's work at his Seattle gallery, says individual drawings have sold there for $5,000 to $20,000. The books in Trusky's safe deposit box collectively contain hundreds of drawings — potentially worth more than Boise State will make from its next bowl appearance.

"It's a remarkably generous gift," Passey said. "But I don't think that for Tom it was about the value. It was about the scholarship."

Tara Burt, Trusky's ex-wife, agreed.

"He lived for books and his passions, so in that sense I'm not surprised that he had them," she said. "But he wouldn't have obtained them for their monetary value. To him it was all about the artistic value."

Half of the books were gifts to Trusky from Castle's late niece, Gerry Garrow. The others he came by in the course of his Castle research.

His will stipulates that their recipient can never sell the books, which BSU almost lost to the Portland Art Museum by waiting until the final day to meet a legal deadline for accepting them.

"If he had only made it a gift to the Broncos, it would have sailed through the uprights," Conley said, "but one of Tom's more endearing quirks was how much he detested football."

He was passionate, however, about Castle's life and art. Trusky spent years researching and writing his 2004 biography of the artist, who grew up in Garden Valley, lived in Star and Boise's Pierce Park area and is buried in Dry Creek Cemetery.

Castle was deaf and couldn't speak or sign. He used pens whittled from sticks and ink made from soot and saliva or leached from colored paper to make drawings and books that have won critical acclaim and graced art periodicals and prestigious galleries.

Castle's books are the most valuable part of Trusky's legacy to the university, but not the only part. He also left his collection of zines and other art books, both worth thousands, and correspondence and other materials that fill a room, six shelves high, in the university's library.

Alan Virta, Boise State's head of special collections, says Trusky's gift "increases our art-books collection fivefold and our zine collection hundreds-fold. He'd hinted that we were going to get his things, but I'm surprised at their extent. I hate to say we don't know what we have, but we don't know what we have yet. It will take years to go through it all.

"... It's a windfall. Not that we'd ever sell any of it, but it's certainly an intellectual windfall."

Mike Ryan, 1952-2009
(Jan. 10, 2010)

The last time my brother-in-law called on a holiday was during that unforgettable moment when BSU was on the edge of beating Oklahoma in the 2007 Fiesta Bowl.

"Tell them to go for two!" he shouted into the phone. "Their defense is exhausted. They've gotta' win it now."

A heart-stopping moment later, they did.

This holiday season, his call came on Christmas Eve.

"I'm going to send you some money," he said.

Something had to be wrong. He was drowning in medical expenses. He didn't have any money.

"Mike, you need money for your medical ..."

"No, Tim. I'm going to die."

Two days later, he did.

The money, we later learned, was a delusion.

We should have known how serious it was when he sent us the T-shirts. They were his treasures, the harvest of a lifetime of collecting. My wife thought he wanted her to make him a Christmas quilt with them, but that wasn't it. He wanted us to keep and wear them. Visible, tactile reminders that he'd existed.

Michael Scott Ryan, "Ry" to his friends, died the day after Christmas at his home in Olympia, Wash. After weeks of struggling for air, he took a last, grateful breath, let it out and was gone. It was the end of three years of suffering as no one should.

If his name is familiar, it's because he was the sick relative I wrote about last January. Statesman readers generously responded, donating more than $5,000 to help with his medical expenses.

Though rarely emotional, he told me one evening how deeply that moved him.

"To think that people who don't even know me would send me money," he said, his voice breaking. "When I'm better, I'm going to write and thank them."

He would have, too. He just never got better.

That most of those who donated didn't know him was their loss. Those who did knew a unique and unforgettable character.

Fifty-seven when he died, he was one of those people who seem eternally youthful. A newspaper production worker, he was a blue-collar guy who loved good beer and good books, pool, motorcycles, hanging out with a seemingly endless array of friends and expounding on politics, current events and sports — about which he was as knowledgeable as he was opinionated.

He umpired baseball games from Little League to semi-pro, was a lifelong fan of the Seattle Mariners and Seahawks, and drolly tolerated other family members' toxic allegiance to the Chicago Cubs. His wit could undo a Carthusian monk. Time and again, I saw him casually start a story and in seconds have everyone in the room crying with laughter, gasping for air and begging him to stop. The remarkable part was that he wasn't trying to be funny. It was natural, spontaneous, deadly.

Late in his life, when they were getting too old to do it themselves, Mike took over his father's former shipmates' job of organizing their annual World War II reunions. They'd served aboard a destroyer sunk by kamikazes, and Mike treated them as the heroes they were. He planned the details of reunions from Seattle to Washington, D.C., escorting the elderly sailors to every event to make sure they were cared for properly.

In 1996, he was diagnosed with a rare blood disorder. At first it seemed to be a simple matter of having a pint of blood removed every few months. What he didn't tell family members, to spare them, was that it was incurable and would get a lot worse.

In the last three years, he had a stem-cell transplant, chemotherapy, anemia, viral infections, rashes, blisters, swollen limbs, near blindness and almost continuous pneumonia. A onetime marathon runner, he lost so much weight he looked like a Holocaust survivor.

One of the few bright spots during that time was the way Statesman readers responded to his suffering. Your generosity, your kindness to a stranger, meant more to him than he was ever able to put down in words. He tried, but he was just too sick.

He wanted you to know that.

Her Own Private Idaho

(Oct. 12, 1993)

Helena Schmidt folds her hands on her lap, studies the view from her home at the end of a dizzying mountain road and considers a question about recent changes in Idaho.

Her response: "What changes?"

An answer worthy of the woman who is one of Idaho's last mountain solitaries. Schmidt lives at Starveout Creek on the Wildhorse River, a peak away from No Business Basin near the edge of Hells Canyon.

From her cabin overlooking the continent's deepest gorge, the pressures of growth and change seem remote. The nearest town, Council, is a two-hour drive. The last six miles take more than an hour, on a private road that would make a mountain goat nervous.

When more people made their livings on isolated mountain ranches, she had 17 neighbors in the Wildhorse River drainage.

Now there are two. The closest is seven miles away.

She lives in the cabin her father built, with logs cut by hand and dragged with a team of horses. Her parents brought her there when she was 10 days old. Except for time in high school at La Grande, Ore., and two years of college, she has spent her life at Starveout Creek. She is 83.

"It's home," she says of her private Idaho. "I have my garden and my rose bushes and my dog and cats. They're my family. ... I hope I never have to live in town."

The words are reminiscent of Buckskin Bill, Frances Wisner and other departed recluses, whose lives in the Idaho wilderness were testimonials to self-reliance. Schmidt's stories are testimonials to how far society has come from the ruggedness that once characterized the West.

When Schmidt was 4 or 5, she fell from a horse and broke her arm. A skilled rider, she climbed back on and rode to the nearest doctor. It took all day.

Her parents were homesteaders and cattle ranchers. She said her father bought the homestead rights to his ranch from Bigfoot John Gerbidge, whose "feet were so big he had to make shoes out of cowhide."

One day a horse knocked her mother down, breaking her leg. Helena had to ride 20 miles alone to get to the nearest telephone. That took all night.

She tells her stories softly, almost shyly, pausing to reflect on harder times from the relative comfort of her home today. Dirt floors have been replaced by polished oak, overalls and chaps by print blouses and earrings. The walls of her cabin are decorated with photos and paintings of the things she knows and loves best — dogs, horses, flowers, mountain scenes.

She has spent most of her life within a few miles of Hells Canyon, never traveling farther than California. The place she would like to see before she dies: the Grand Canyon.

Visitors use words like "paradise" and "Shangri-la" to describe her 110 acres, which lie in a hollow surrounded by virgin timber and mountains of heart-stopping immensity.

Her rolling lawn is lined with flower gardens and shaded by red cedar and white fir trees. Coyotes howl from the peaks.

There is little of which she is afraid. Bears and snakes are regular visitors; she kills rattlesnakes with a hoe.

"I'm only afraid of people," she says. "And I'm not that afraid of them."

Schmidt's introduction to society came late. Her mother taught her at home for three years. When she was 10, she entered the fourth grade in the one-room school down the mountain on the other side of Wildhorse River.

To get there, students had to walk a log across the water. In winter, the log was icy. Schmidt remembers drying out by the school's potbellied stove the time she fell and broke her arm.

After high school, she earned a teaching certificate at what is now Western Washington University in Bellingham, Wash.

"They've changed the name?" she asked, her eyes widening. "It used to just be Bellingham Normal."

She spent two years teaching in a one-room school at Brownlee, riding a horse four hours each way to help her parents on weekends. Brownlee's enrollment fell from 10 students her first year to five the second. The school closed that spring for lack of students.

Helena Moore and Henry Schmidt met at a dance in Bear, Idaho, and were married when she was 27. She helped build their home — she calls it a shack — down Starveout Creek from her parents' house. After her parents died, she and Henry moved into the sturdier home.

For three decades, she helped run cattle at their ranch and others, sleeping on the ground, living in shacks and tents, doing whatever had to be done to put food on the table.

She was a top hand before it was considered proper for women to work in the fields. She rode, roped, fed cattle, milked cows, cut and bucked hay, drove a team, ran a mowing machine.

Her father died in 1939, her mother in 1947. In 1963, she and Henry retired. Five years later, Henry died.

Living alone "was hard in a way, but not in the sense that I needed things done for me."

The hard part was the grief, the loneliness and getting older.

In 1979, at age 69, she made an agreement with neighbors Ralph and Dodie Brown. They built a cabin behind hers and signed a contract making them responsible for maintaining the property and looking after Schmidt, who has no children. In exchange, they will own it after she dies. She said the property was last appraised in 1979, at $100,000.

Life on Starveout Creek, named about 1900 after a couple failed to receive a winter's supply of food, is easier now, but hardly citified. It's a two-hour drive to get mail or groceries. She buys gasoline a ton at a time, in 50-gallon drums carried in the back of her Chevrolet pickup. Her two-story cabin is heated with wood. Water is heated on a woodstove or propane stove. Fruit and vegetables are canned over an open fire.

In winter, months pass without visitors or trips to town. She has seen snow four feet deep on the level and weathered subzero temperatures and 70 mph winds.

At 83, Schmidt remains largely self-reliant. She raises chickens, maintains a large vegetable garden and berry patch, cans fruit from the trees that dot the lawn around her cabin. She has four cows and is more than a little indignant that none is giving milk.

"I guess the bull wasn't any good," she explains. "It's the first time I've been without a milk cow, and it's no way to be."

She says it would be nice to have "real electricity."

"I'd like to be able to run the lights without having to run the generator for hours to charge up the batteries. ... I don't use my mixer. It's easier to use the eggbeater than it is to start the generator."

In 1978, the Cambridge Telephone Co. hired a family to install a phone line.

"It's nice to be able to talk to someone now and then," she said. "... It didn't used to get lonesome for me, but it has been since I've been widowed."

When she gets bored, she works in her garden or goes for a walk with Ruff, her border collie.

"He's very protective," she says.

To relax, she listens to fiddle music on the radio, plays solitaire, crochets, knits, makes quilts and reads. Her taste in reading runs to crafts and homemaking magazines, James Michner and books on gardening, nutrition and home remedies.

She doesn't go to church (the road would keep a saint away) and doesn't consider herself religious, but there are four Bibles on her bookshelves.

Her advice for living:

"Do unto others. I don't know of anything better than that."

Her advice for those who want to escape the pressures of modern times:

"Well, I wouldn't want them all to come to Starveout," she says, pausing longer than usual to think about it.

"But I guess that would be the way to do it."

Editor's note: Schmidt's home burned down on March 8, 1998, and was rebuilt by neighbors. She died Nov. 1, 2000, when her car slid off the edge of the mountain-goat road. She was 90.

A Lifetime of Trees
(April 23, 1991)

OWYHEE COUNTY – When Garfield Shults was a kid growing up in the shadow of the Tetons, where the snow can be 20 feet deep, he spent winter evenings studying tree catalogs and dreaming of spring.

"They had all these catalogs then with red, juicy, dripping plums and luscious peaches and other things we couldn't grow in East Idaho because the growing season was so short," he recalled. "The gardening bug went real deep into me. Now I can't get away from it."

Not that he's tried. Shults's home west of Homedale is a one-man tree exhibit. Signs – "Garfield Shults, Trees" — dot the countryside for miles. Trees surround the little white house where he lives with his cat and his catalogs, fill the 38 acres of rolling land he has owned for more than 40 years.

He has Scotch pines, nut pines, Jeffrey pines, ponderosa pines.

He has peaches, plums, apricots, cherries, apples.

He has walnuts, heartnuts, buartnuts, butternuts, filberts, hazelberts.

He has hickories, persimmons, quince, plumcots (plums and apricots growing from the same tree). He has peaches and plums growing from the same tree, cherries and plums on the same tree, apricots and prunes on the same tree.

In a state where subzero temperatures are common, he once had palm trees.

Today his most unusual specimen is a tree with seven different kinds of pecans.

Pecans are generally considered southern trees, but in 1980 Shults found a variety that would survive Idaho winters. He carefully grafted other varieties to it, and last summer filled two gallon buckets with nuts most commonly produced in Georgia.

The equivalent would be growing Idaho russets in the everglades.

Even in the South, it usually takes 17 to 20 years for a pecan tree to begin to bear. Shults cut the time to six years.

He is a very good gardener.

People have come from as far away as California, where he once taught gardening, to see his trees and ask him questions. Some offer to pay for tours of his property, which is scattered with tools, woodpiles, old cars. An ancient, powder-blue truck with "here's peaches" painted on the hood slumbers beside the house.

Shults doesn't just sell fruit; he sells trees themselves. (Look for Homedale to become the Atlanta West of the pecan industry.) He also sells parts of trees, shipping twigs from the more unusual varieties to a tree company in Missouri.

One of his favorites, an unusual variety of cherry growing on the hillside overlooking his home, is now the parent of 5,400 trees sold nationwide.

"I keep giving the company ideas on how to advertise it, and they say not to worry about it," he said. "They can't keep up with the demand as it is."

At 68, Garfield Shults remains a man literally in love with trees. After growing them virtually all his life (his first "crop" was 11 cherries from a tree he planted when he was 16), he still is experimenting with new techniques, still looks forward to each year's harvest.

I asked him whether, after more than half a century of working with trees, there were any kinds he didn't have but still wanted.

"Yes," he said, "but you can't get them to grow here.

"I've always wanted to have a pistachio tree."

Nellie and the Mailman
(June 26, 1980)

Wilbur Yorkovich drives the stage to Atlanta, a community of 20 at the edge of the Sawtooth Mountains. He leaves the main post office in Boise about 7:30 a.m., drops the bulk of the mail at the one-room Atlanta post office around lunchtime and gets back to Boise in the afternoon, usually between 4 and 4:30. He is a punctual man.

Like many backcountry residents, the patrons of Yorkovich's route are eager for the sound of another human voice; they welcome their mailman with coffee, pastries, even fish-head soup. Like many backcountry mail carriers, Yorkovich is eager for the road. He enjoys the conversation, but a mailman has a schedule to keep.

"I think the world of these folks," he said, "but when I have to go I have to go. ... Once I was getting up to leave some people's house, and they said, 'Hey, you're getting better. You stayed 10 minutes this time.'"

Yorkovich is 54 and has driven the route 11 years. It's just an ordinary dirt road, but to him every mile is a memory.

"A lot of memories," he says, "and a lot of good people."

He points to the place where he refused to pull a car off an embankment because its owner was too drunk to drive. He remembers where he taught a stranded traveler how to change a tire, the piece of road where he stepped on 14 baby rattlesnakes, the spot where he stopped to talk to a newborn fawn. He knows where the deer lose their footing and split their bellies on the ice of a frozen reservoir; he shows you where the Forest Service has bulldozed the cabins of his friends.

"There's where Nellie's store was," he said as we approached a grove of trees. "Right there in those trees."

The store was bulldozed in 1977. Today a ring of blackened campfire rocks is the only indication that anyone spent time there. Nothing is left to commemorate the story of Wilbur and Nellie.

Nellie Hirt was the mailman's friend. Her Last Chance Grocery really was the last chance, before Atlanta, to pick up snacks and cold drinks.

Nellie made everyone who stopped sign a guest register. Not everyone got what he stopped for.

"One day while I was stopped there a guy came in and wanted to buy a six-pack of beer," Yorkovich said. "Nellie asked how many people were with him. 'Just two of us,' the guy said. 'Then I'll sell you two bottles of beer,' Nellie said. And that's all she'd sell him. Any more than that and she figured it wasn't safe to drive this road. That's just the way she was."

Nellie was in her 70s and had operated the store for years when Yorkovich took the mail route in 1969. As she grew older, she complained of respiratory problems and poor circulation.

"She kept saying her feet hurt," he said. "I brought her everything I could think of, but nothing seemed to help, so one day I told her to get ready and on my way back I'd take her to town. I told her she could see the doctor, stay the night with me and Mama (Yorkovich's wife) and I'd drive her back the next day. She said she would, but when I got back she wasn't ready. She said she didn't want to leave."

Leaving home, even for a night, was a touchy subject. Nellie wouldn't even leave to take money to the bank. She kept her business proceeds in a cigar box. When the box was full, she gave it to Yorkovich and asked him to deposit the money to her account.

Time passed, her health worsened, Yorkovich made another offer. He would take a day off, drive her to a doctor, and bring her back home the same day.

It didn't work out. Two doctors said there was nothing they could do unless she was admitted to a hospital. She refused; the doctors asked Yorkovich to sign the admitting papers.

"I couldn't do it," he said. "I told them that if I did that, that woman'd never speak to me again."

As the months passed, the man who hates to stop for more than a few minutes stopped long enough to cut the old woman's firewood. She had stopped eating, so he stayed mornings to give her breakfast and make sure she ate it. His wife cooked meals; he delivered them with the mail. He brought her medicine and stayed until she took it. He paid for the medicine himself.

One day the mailman knocked and didn't get an answer. Then, from inside the store, a voice cried for help.

"I heard her saying, 'Please don't leave me alone.' She was lying on the floor hemorrhaging. The fire was out and it was cold. The boss was with me that day, and we put her in bed and built a fire. Then we radioed to Idaho City and got a helicopter to take her to Boise."

After 10 days of intensive care, the 82-year-old woman who wouldn't leave the mountains for a single night was transferred to a Boise nursing home. She died within a week and was buried in a Boise cemetery.

"She was somethin'," Yorkovich said as we hurried past the trees and blackened rocks, right on schedule. He looked the other way, out the side window, as he spoke. It might have been the dust, or it might have been the smoke from his cigarette, but his eyes were shining as they turned back to the road he knows so well.

Desert Dog Whisperer
(Aug. 2, 2004)

Tish and Teal. (Kim Hughes / Idaho Statesman)

OWYHEE COUNTY — Tish Lewis swears she's not a dog trainer.

"Goodness, don't call me that," she says with her proper British accent. "I'm not a dog trainer. I'm a groom."

She was, in fact, one of the world's top horse grooms. (She met Queen Elizabeth in a horse barn.) But to crowds watching her work her border collies at the Western Idaho Fair, Ketchum's Trailing of the Sheep festival and other events, the differences between Lewis and a professional trainer are academic.

Teal, the top dog on the Lewis ranch, is 10 and has been working with Lewis since she was 3. Teal doesn't actually speak English; Lewis just makes it look that way.

"Come by," she says softly.

Teal moves nine pastured sheep to the left.

"Away," Lewis says.

The dog moves the sheep to the right.

"She used to do perfectly square turns," Lewis says, almost apologetically. "But she's getting older and I don't get on her about it."

That said, she blows softly on a crescent-shaped whistle she wears around her neck. Teal separates four sheep from the flock and lets them return to the barn. The five that are left try to follow, but the dog holds them where they are. With the sheep getting edgier by the second, Teal looks at Lewis. Her eyes are canine question marks.

"OK," Lewis says. With a silent communication understood only by animals, and perhaps Lewis, Teal allows the sheep to leave.

"Teal, that'll do."

"That'll do" is the equivalent of a 5 o'clock whistle. Her work done, the border collie trots to her master's side.

The granddaughter of a British international champion, Teal appears to herd the sheep effortlessly.

"People think sheep are stupid, but they aren't," Lewis said. "They're very smart. They can size up a dog in an instant. A dog has to have the power in its eyes. Some have it, some don't. If they don't, the sheep won't do anything for them. I'm lucky with Teal."

The skill of the handler also is a factor, one that makes Lewis a crowd pleaser wherever she works her dogs for audiences. Though she'd never refer to herself as a "whisperer," she's a natural at communicating with animals.

"She understands how animals think," Caldwell dog trainer Don Helsley said. "She learned that from working with horses. And she's always happy, so everything ends in a positive way, and her dogs are always willing to work for her."

Patrick Shannahan of Caldwell, a winner of the U.S. Border Collie Handlers Association's national competition, agreed.

"To do what Tish does, you have to be able to read animals," Shannahan said. "She knows how to read dogs and sheep and how her communication with the dog is affecting the sheep. Whether it be dogs or sheep or horses, she's a wonderful animal person."

Lewis doesn't remember a time when she wasn't an animal person. She grew up in England and Wales and attended an agricultural college near London. By then her lifelong interest in horses, dogs and sheep was well-established.

"From the time I was little, I always wanted to ride," she said. "Kids were evacuated to Wales during World War II, and I got interested in sheep there. I think it was because there were so many of them there and because I liked to see the dogs work with them."

She emigrated to Canada in her late 20s and became an instructor and manager at a stable and riding school in Vancouver, B.C. She was there when Queen Elizabeth II and her husband, Prince Phillip, came to visit. The stable's cutting horses impressed the prince so much he decided to have them shipped to England for a tour there. Lewis was invited to go along as the groom, the person who cares for the horses. She was in a barn in England with her head in a tack trunk when an unexpected visitor arrived.

"I was getting the horses ready when I heard a car drive up," she said. "I looked up from the tack trunk and here was the queen! She drove herself, which surprised me. She asked me about the horses and how I fed them and other things about their care. She was nice and very interested. She and her people are all horse people. ...

"Prince Phillip was a real kick. He told us one day that 'you girls take better care of your horses than you do your husbands.' "

At risk of offending the prince with a correction, Lewis refrained from mentioning that she wasn't married. Animals had been her life, and she was rarely in one place for long. Her work took her to Canada, England, New Zealand and the United States, where, among other things, she won carriage-driving championships and met her future husband.

Gene Lewis was a former Owyhee County buckaroo who had achieved international fame as a jumping horse rider and trainer. She worked for him for years and, at age 53, married him. They spent 17 years in California before moving to Idaho in 1995. Gene wanted to be closer to his roots. For his wife, accustomed to abundant rainfall and lush greenery, Owyhee County might as well have been the moon.

"There was nothing out here," she said. "No electricity, not a tree, nothing. I often wonder what my mother would think of me living out here. She probably would have thought this was the back of beyond. But I love it now. I don't go into town unless I run out of milk."

Their ranch home is decorated with tack, memorabilia from a lifetime of working with horses — and drawings of horses, sheep and dogs.

"I've spent most of my life working with horses," she said, "but I'm 72 now and don't move quick enough to work with those big horses anymore. I'd have to say I've come to enjoy the dogs more. Wherever I've lived, I've had a dog. They've always been a part of my life, and they always will be."

This is Tough
(May 19, 2003)

BRUNEAU — Rodeo champion Jan Youren reduces to a single word the thing that has kept her in the tough-as-nails world of bareback riding longer than anyone.

"It's not upper-body strength," she said. "It's not even balance or adrenaline, even though they're important. It's what my daddy would call fortitude."

Fortitude has helped Youren win five world championships as a bareback bronc rider. It has helped her ride 2,000-pound bulls and compete with injuries that would sideline most NFL players. And it's a big part of what still makes her one of the top bareback riders in the country — at age 59.

No other bareback rider in the world — man or woman — has competed as long. Her staying power has put the Garden Valley native in the National Cowgirl Hall of Fame and made her a rodeo icon.

"I know of one cowboy, Freckles Brown, who was in the national finals when he was 50," Snake River Stampede executive secretary Jimmie Hurley said. "Everybody thought that was incredible, but it doesn't hold a candle to what Jan's done and how long and how well she's done it. She takes falls you'd think would half kill her and jumps up and runs out of the arena like an 18-year-old. She's just amazing."

Most female rodeo riders compete in roping or barrel racing instead of the male-dominated rough-stock events of bull riding and bareback riding. Fewer than 20 people comprise the bareback circuit of the Women's Professional Rodeo Association. Most are in their early 20s.

The nation's No. 2 bareback rider in the most recent standings is 20-year-old Tasha Stevenson of Wheatland, Wyo. — Youren's granddaughter.

"This craziness is inherited," Bruneau's 59-year-old cowgirl said. "It can't be helped."

She halfheartedly says this could be her last year before retiring to the more sedate world of barrel racing. No one believes her.

"I've heard that before," granddaughter Tavia Stevenson, Tasha's 19-year-old sister, said with a chuckle. "It would be nice in a way because I hate seeing her hit the ground. She gets in some pretty good wrecks, and you wonder if she's going to be all right. On the other hand, it wouldn't be the same without her."

Youren hits the ground every time she rides. A successful ride lasts six seconds before a "picket man" transfers the rider from her bucking horse to his horse. For the past four years, Youren hasn't been able to use a picket man. Her shoulders have been dislocated so many times she can't reach out to put her arms around him.

"I know I'm going to hit the dirt," she said. "It's just a question of how hard."

She rode most of the 1987 season, and won the world title that year, with her back broken. She's broken her back twice. She's broken her collarbone, both arms, both wrists, five vertebrae in her neck and all but one of her ribs. Her cheekbones have been broken eight times, her nose 14 times.

She's had scalp lacerations, multiple concussions and more than 200 stitches — and somehow doesn't look like a train wreck. White hair frames a face with lively blue eyes, a straight nose and almost no scars.

Jim, her husband of 19 years, said he worries about her "a little bit. But it's her life, and I'm not going to interfere. I don't tell her to go, and I don't tell her to stay home."

Cole Youren, their 18-year-old son, worries "until she hits the ground. Then I know she's OK."

After being knocked out by a horse that ran over her at a rodeo in Tucson, Ariz., Youren tried to put a rope on the wrong end of a bull. Early the next morning, family members found her climbing into a car filled with men she'd never seen before. She was still only semi-conscious. X-rays showed that her brain was swollen.

"It could have been worse," she said with a straight face. "I only got hit by three of the hooves."

Tavia Stevenson agrees about the inherited craziness. Her grandmother gave up riding bulls after 33 years when she realized that "the bulls were on top of me more than I was on top of them."

Tavia Stevenson's liver was lacerated when a bull stepped on her.

"I was riding in the world's toughest rodeos, and the doctor told me to wait five to six months before I even got on a goat or I could die," she said.

Youren was concerned enough that she pulled her granddaughter out of the competition. Equipped with a special belt to hold her liver in place, Tavia Stevenson was back in action five weeks later at a rodeo in Lincoln, Neb. A Lincoln radio announcer who commented on her toughness was taken aback by Tavia Stevenson's response:

"I'm not tough at all. Tough is Jan Youren."

Youren's rodeo career began when her father, a legendary Garden Valley tough guy named Sterling Alley, produced Idaho's first all-girls rodeo in Emmett. Daughter Jan, then 12, was among the contestants. She initially came in third, but drew the most fearsome horse in the county for a re-ride.

"I came down and plowed a furrow you could have planted a potato crop in," she said. "Daddy used to introduce my sisters and me as his pretty daughter, his crazy daughter, his sweet daughter and his baby daughter. You can guess which one I was."

She won $54 at Emmett's all-girls rodeo, thought she was on the road to riches and says she's still looking for it 48 years later.

Her longevity has made her a celebrity. She's been a guest on "To Tell the Truth," the Maury Povich show and "Late Night with Conan O'Brien."

She's turned down David Letterman three times, she said.

"I met him at a rodeo in Cheyenne, and he rubbed me the wrong way. He was talkin' down to people. I don't think I could be very nice to him."

Celebrity notwithstanding, the road to riches remains elusive. Top rodeo cowboys can win $150,000 per event at their national finals. Winners at the Women's National Finals Rodeo, held in Fort Worth, Texas, in November, earn $6,800. Purses at the roughly 30 Women's Professional Rodeo Association rodeos leading up to the finals can be as small as $200.

"You can't be in it for the money," said Youren, who runs a cattle ranch near Bruneau with her husband and works part-time as a flagger for the Idaho Department of Transportation. "Even if I win, those little bitty purses don't pay for my gas."

The women's circuit includes rodeos as far away as Florida and Pennsylvania. Youren drives 60,000 to 70,000 miles a year in her 4-year-old Ford pickup. Her backup "outfits" are a 1994 Lincoln with more than 300,000 miles on its odometer and a 20-year-old GMC van she uses when she hauls passengers. To cut costs, she and her competitors travel together whenever possible and share expenses. Her traveling companions frequently include her Wyoming granddaughters and their mother, Tonya Stevenson, still competing at age 42.

Grandma is "ornery and likes to pick on us — she's always giving us wet Willies and stuff — but she's fun to be around," Tavia Stevenson said. "We have a lot of good times on the road."

Youren is a mentor to nearly everyone on the circuit. She teaches bareback riding — students have come to her Bruneau ranch from as far away as West Virginia — and she figures she's helped 80 to 90 percent of her competitors get started.

"I like to think about what I'm doing and not have anybody talk to me before I ride," Tavia Stevenson said. "She can go around helping everybody, and when it's her time to ride, she just jumps on and goes.

"... I think the thing that makes her so good is she really loves it. She never quits, and she's got a good attitude about it. She gives it her best, but she doesn't take it too seriously. She gets up smiling even when she doesn't do well."

What keeps her going?

She said without hesitation that it's the six magical seconds on the back of a bucking horse. A 6-second thrill most people can only imagine.

"I don't do drugs, but I'm sure there's no drug that could give you a bigger high. It's kind of like a dance in a way. When you have a good ride, there's nothing else like it."

Riding is her reward, an escape from the pressures of running a farm and raising a big family — eight children, 61 grandchildren and 10 great-grandchildren.

"I hate to think of all the hours I've spent on football bleachers or at basketball games or cooking family dinners. This is what I do for me. It's my recreation."

Immersed in the ranch's spring branding, she reminisced as she worked.

"I've had a full life," she said, flipping a calf on its side as easily as if it were a puppy. "I've packed about everything into it that I could have wanted."

Cole, the last of her children still at home, gripped the branding iron and waited for instructions.

"Higher," she said. "There."

The calf bawled; pungent smoke narrowed the eyes of everyone but the rodeo champ. After all her breaks and cuts and bruises, she seems almost immune to pain.

"If I end up in a wheelchair, I've deserved it," she said. "I won't be bitter or nasty about it. I'm the luckiest woman in the world. I've got a ton of kids and grandkids, and I'll have stories for all of them."

Inventor Extraordinaire
(July 27, 1998)

Harold Hannebaum with one of his many inventions, a solar-heated hot tub and exercise pool. (Katherine Jones / Idaho Statesman)

BELLEVUE — High as he is on his newest brainstorm, Harold Hannebaum stops short of calling it the invention of a lifetime. He's only 88. Anything is possible.

One of Bellevue's best-kept secrets, Hannebaum has been inventing things since he was a kid growing up in Indiana. The first was a contraption to dry the linen line on his father's fishing reel. He was 7.

At 14, he invented a cigarette-vending machine. People paid double the going rate to watch it work.

In his 30s, he invented a glass fireplace. It made him rich.

Fast forward 50 more years, to a sweltering afternoon at his home in Bellevue. Hannebaum crouches over a jug of gasoline with a frayed green hose running to the exhaust pipe of his 1978 Lincoln Continental. The Lincoln idles as he drops burning matches into the gas. A passerby would think he was trying to commit suicide.

"Are you sure it's in right?" his wife, Tillie, asks as flames scamper up the hose.

"I think it's good enough," he says, swatting a hot spot on the sleeve of his Western shirt.

"I don't want you to think. I want you to be damned sure."

Half a dozen matches later, he's made his point: Only the fumes exposed to air outside the jug burned.

"If the jug had oxygen in it instead of carbon monoxide from the exhaust, it would have gone sky high," he said. "The Lincoln would have gone along for the ride."

The theory is the basis of his latest invention, an explosion-resistant fuel tank. He got the idea after TWA Flight 800 exploded. The U.S. Patent office approved his patent-pending application last week.

His inventions number more than 400. They dot the grounds and fill unexpected spaces of the Hannebaums' rambling Bellevue home: a hunting motorcycle and copper still in the basement, a solar-heated pool in the exercise room, an alcohol-powered truck in the front yard, an ancient lawnmower in the back yard.

He made the mower with a tractor wheel rim, washing machine motor, hay mower blade and wheels from a welding cart and kiddy car. That was in the 1940s. His neighbors liked it so well he made mowers for them. As far as he knows, his was the first rotary lawnmower. He never thought to get a patent.

It looks like a used-parts collection and sounds like a threshing machine, but it works. A board dangling from the back keeps a tempest of grass and dust from enveloping him as he cuts the lawn.

"It's the only mower I've ever had," he says, his blue eyes shining. "I've never bought a mower in my life."

The first decade of his life was a Huckleberry Finn idyll on an Indiana tobacco farm. His family moved to Gooding when he was 10. His first Idaho invention, at 11, was a side-delivery hay rake for tractors.

He used to keep his ideas in a shoe box, but switched to a suitcase when he hit 200. His inventions cover the spectrum from self-cooling dimmer switches and self-aligning doors to heat-holding pot covers, weapons and assorted models of his biggest seller, the Carousel glass fireplace. He invented it in 1949, patented it in 1966, got lucky in 1967.

"It surprised the hell out of me," he said. "A fellow came to the door one day and said he wanted to look at our fireplace. He looked at it and took notes for about an hour. Then he called a guy in California. He flew up here that night, looked at our fireplace for two hours and asked if I'd mind if he manufactured it. I told him I wouldn't mind a bit."

The guy from California, Glen Crownover of Malm Fireplace Manufacturers, sold more than 50,000 of the circular fireplaces with the spinning flames. Hannebaum hasn't worried about money since.

Richard Hooper, publisher of "Who's Who of American Inventors," says Hannebaum is an exception:

"I've never met a rich inventor. Inventing is a disease. If I can catch a person before he gets the disease, I'll talk him out of it because there's a lot easier ways to make a living. Very few inventors are successful."

Of inventors competing for some 100,000 patents a year, Hooper said, 15 percent are independents. "Who's Who" recognizes a small percentage of the 15 percent. Hannebaum is one of them.

He also plays the banjo, guitar and harmonica, sings Elvis songs, splits wood, writes poetry and is the author of a folksy, seven-volume autobiography, "The Adventures of Indiana Hannebaum." The University of Idaho Press has published the first two volumes.

The Hannebaums have no children. Book royalties and most of their estate will fund scholarships for American Indians, because Harold thinks "they got a raw deal."

Larry Christensen, of San Marcos, Calif., helped set up the scholarship fund at Idaho State University. He also set up a Hannebaum Web site: members.aol.com/lhchristen/index.htm

"I did it because I want more people to learn about him," Christensen said. "He's just such a natural inventor. He sees a problem and goes right to the heart of it. I think he's a national treasure."

Craig Korfanta, Hannebaum's Boise patent attorney, calls him "the epitome of the attic inventor. He's the stereotypical American dreamer, and he's been very successful at it."

Few would guess. The Hannebaums live quietly in a modest home on a shady street on a ragged edge of Bellevue. They drive a 20-year-old car because they don't think the new ones have enough zip. They used to travel the world. Now they're content to stay home.

"I hate it when he wants us to go somewhere," Tillie said. "My favorite thing is just being home with Harold."

They spent five years remodeling and enlarging their home. Lights with colored bulbs burn in its heavily draped rooms on even the brightest days. Fourteen framed patents outline a dimly lit doorway. Glass fireplaces and pictures of Elvis seem to be everywhere. One end of the living room is a combination solarium and pet cemetery.

"Our birds are buried there," Tillie said. "Burl Ives, Tillie Bird and Zippy."

At 88 and 70, the Hannebaums flirt like playful teen-agers. They pepper their conversations with provocative quips, affectionate compliments, laughter.

They met when Harold came to her parents' farm near Gooding to look at a cow. Tillie caught his eye instead. Her father gave them the cow as a wedding present.

Fifty-two years later, they still act like newlyweds. She still calls him Haroldy.

Haroldy runs a mile to the mailbox and back every day. He cuts and splits the wood that helps heat their home in the fireplaces he invented, chins himself on the monkey bars in the solar-heated exercise pool he built. With his Western tie, Elvis sideburns and Grand Prix bicycle racing cap, he looks positively rakish.

His eyes sparkle when he describes his next invention, a device to keep snow from accumulating on the windshields of 18-wheelers.

"Inventing," he says when asked what keeps him young. "Doing what you like and being what you are."

Historian Emeritus
(May 15, 2000)

It's a bittersweet observation heard increasingly in Idaho: Not even Bill Gates can build a computer capable of downloading Merle Wells's memory.

"Nobody makes a computer that big," said Ron Bush, chairman of the Idaho Historical Society's Board of Trustees. "But someone needs to figure out a way to save his knowledge of Idaho and Pacific Northwest history before it's lost. What's inside his head is irreplaceable."

Acclaim for Wells's encyclopedic knowledge is reaching new levels as his health, never robust, worsens. His recent honors include a National Park Service award, the newly completed Merle W. Wells State Archives

Building and a tribute in the new edition of the Idaho Highway Historical Marker Guide.

Idaho's historian emeritus — no one else has held the title — Wells spent much of this month and last in radiation therapy at St. Luke's Regional Medical Center before being transferred last week to a Boise nursing home.

The cancer first diagnosed 10 years ago in his prostate is spreading to other parts of his body; the prognosis is uncertain.

"I could be around for quite a while or for not very long at all," he said. "We did look at cemetery plots up at Dry Creek. They have some good deals there. But I'm not in any hurry to jump into one."

If there was a common bond among the visitors to Wells's bedside, it's a shared belief that the frail figure with wisps of white hair caressing his blue hospital gown knows more than anyone else is ever likely to know about Idaho history. Other noted historians are among his unabashed admirers. Many consider him a living treasure.

"I don't think the people of Idaho appreciate what a resource he's been," State Historian Larry Jones said. "There probably hasn't been any history of Idaho written in the last 50 years that doesn't have his thumbprint on it in one way or another."

The man people respectfully call "Dr. Wells" wrote the legislation creating the state archives and the majority of the texts for the state's 244 historical highway markers. He helped begin county and city historical societies and commissions throughout the state. He has written nine historical books and more than 100 scholarly articles on Idaho and regional history. He was the state preservation officer for parts of three decades. For nearly half a century, in positions from director to unpaid volunteer, he has been the heart and soul of the Idaho Historical Society.

"He's my tutor and greatest teacher," said Arthur Hart, the society's director emeritus. "When I was teaching in the East, I was invited to a lunch at the Harvard Club (with a group of noted historians). They all agreed that when it came to Idaho and Northwest history, Merle

Wells was the final authority. Historians far beyond Idaho regard him as something special."

He also is regarded as a character as colorful as those who inhabit the pages of the historical books he has authored. Until recently, Wells was a familiar sight on the streets of Boise, negotiating rush-hour traffic on a hot-pink girl's bicycle. He is equally known for weaving historical tales that are hours or days in the telling, and for tearing across rugged terrain in his battered pickup at speeds that defy belief.

He likes straw hats and Shakespeare, Mom and Pop cafes and lemon meringue pie, the music of Bach and Beethoven, collecting stamps and taking pictures with his vintage Leica camera. But his passion is regional history. His knowledge of Territorial Idaho is so detailed that he gives the impression of having been there. His signature phrase — drawled, not spoken: "Well, that's not e-x-a-c-t-l-y the way it happened."

Then he explains the way it did happen. Exactly.

A staple of the Wells approach to history is to see the places where it happened. There is virtually no corner of the state he hasn't trod.

Retired archivist Gary Bettis learned the extent of his former boss's knowledge as many have, traveling the state with the loquacious Wells behind the wheel.

"One of the things that sets him apart among historians is his inclusiveness," Bettis said. "He not only knows events in Idaho history better than anyone else has ever known them, but he also knows the factors leading up to them nationally and internationally. He knows the entire context. We were at the top of the Horseshoe Bend hill once when I asked him a question. He'd digress once in a while, but generally he was wrapping up the story as we were pulling into Coeur d'Alene."

Wells's driving — he has a penchant for impulsively steering toward whatever interests him — is legendary. One unsuspecting passenger was George Vogt, now director of the State Historical Society of Wisconsin.

"I was visiting Boise working for the National Archives when I met Merle, who is one of the more truly amazing people I've ever known," he said. "We were driving from Boise to Helena (Montana) for a meeting, and the staff chuckled and said they'd put me in a car with him. I quickly learned that one thing you want to do when you're traveling in the mountains with Merle is tell him you want to drive. That way he can talk, and you don't have to worry about him driving off the road.

"He talked about history, the flora and fauna, the geography — his knowledge was totally comprehensive. We took detours to see ruts of the Oregon Trail and the Stanley Basin, and he knew everything there was to know about everything we saw. It was the most delightful eight-hour drive I've ever taken. It was absolutely wonderful, and I'll never forget it."

At 81, Wells still has a reputation for rarely forgetting anything.

"On one of my visits to Boise we were having a long conversation about historical records management and got interrupted, and ultimately I had to leave town," Vogt said. "Two years later, I ran into him at a national meeting, and he said, 'Now, as I was saying … And he picked up the conversation from two years earlier as if we'd never left off."

Routine details are another story. Jan Jones, who owns a beauty shop in the downtown apartment building where Wells lived for many years, remembers him approaching her late one evening to say he was leaving on a trip and was a little short.

"He said he was going to Europe the next morning and forgot to go to the bank," she said. "He wanted to know if maybe he could write me a check to get some cash. When I asked him how much he needed, he looked in his wallet, said he had $20 and figured another $100 would do it. He was going to Europe on $120."

Larry Jones calls Wells "the most frugal employee the state of Idaho ever had. When we traveled, we slept out a lot. He was always looking for ways to save money. If we needed a four-wheel-drive, he'd find one for $400. We were down in Wyoming in one of them when the camper shell fell off. Then we couldn't get the transmission out of first gear. So here we are going down the highway with the camper shell roped on, and bicycles are passing us.

"Merle was unflappable. He said that going 5 mph gave us a good chance to get a feel for the country."

Wells's interest in history began early. His father, who later would become a speaker of the Idaho House of Representatives, was part of a group of Idahoans the Canadian Pacific Railroad recruited to develop farmland in Alberta. The first of Norman and Minnie Wells's two sons was born in Lethbridge, Alberta, in 1918 and raised as a U.S. national in an ever-changing succession of Canadian schools.

"My parents moved 16 times in 12 years, so I remember a lot of different things from a lot of different places there," he said. "We were part of a small colony of people who were opening up that part of the West. A lot of my later interests grew out of that."

Seeking better economic opportunities, the family moved to Boise in 1930.

A teacher, Minnie Wells wanted her boys to experience the benefits of life in a city. They lived in a two-story house with a big front porch at 1210 N. 22nd St. As a fifth-grader at Lowell School, 12-year-old Merle was surprised to find substantial differences between Canadian and American education.

"Here, George Washington was a hero," he said. "Up there, he was 'that old traitor.' The only common connection with the War of 1812 was that it happened in 1812. It taught me that there's always another side to the story. As a historian, you have to be skeptical."

Seamlessly, the professor takes charge. He drops historical nuggets as effortlessly as his listeners drop their jaws.

"Speaking of the War of 1812, did you know the White House came out of all that? The British forces damaged it and much of Washington in retaliation for our invaders damaging York. It was painted white when it was redone, and that's how we got the White House."

In elementary school, the future Ph.D. was a slow starter. At or near the bottom of his class, he lost sleep worrying about his grades until his sixth-grade teacher identified the problem.

"I didn't know till sixth grade that you were supposed to be able to read what was on the blackboard. I was aware that things were there, but couldn't read them. Once they figured it out that I'd be better off if

I could see what was on the board, they got me glasses, and I began to come along."

As an honor student at Boise High School, Boise Junior College and the College of Idaho, the young Wells came along in exemplary fashion. He planned to study law until BJC President Eugene Chaffee suggested a master's program in history, preparatory to law, at the University of California at Berkeley. The cost was $160, coincidentally the total of Wells's savings. He earned his board by waiting tables at the Presbyterian student center.

It was a year that would cost Idaho a lawyer. Armed with his master's degree, he taught for four years at the C of I, returned to Berkeley for his doctorate, and the rest was history.

A lifelong bachelor, he says he "thought I'd probably marry and have a family, but it didn't happen."

Life after Berkeley was a 6-year stint as an associate professor of history at a college in Pennsylvania, but Idaho remained in his heart. He returned to Boise as a consulting historian for the Idaho State Historical Society in 1956. In 1959, the society's first professional director, Jerry Swinney, hired him as historian and archivist.

"It was fortunate for me, because I knew nothing about the history of Idaho and ran into the man who knew more about it than anyone," said Swinney, now retired and living in Rochester, N.Y. "He had written his master's and doctoral theses on subjects of Idaho history, and formal scholarship was a matter of personal importance to him.

"We used to travel together a lot. His only concession to hot weather was unbuttoning his cuffs. He knew every place in Idaho you could get to in a car or truck and everything about it once you got there. I don't have an advanced degree, but I've always felt I have the equivalent of a Ph.D. from Merle. All my life, I've dealt with graduate-trained historians and have always felt on even terms with them because of what I learned from him."

Wells valued his hard-won education, but didn't let it set him apart. Stephanie Toothman, a regional coordinator with the National Park Service, discovered his Everyman side while they were traveling the state together, documenting historical sites.

"I've walked into the most obscure places and seen him greeted by name and a piece of pie cut before we ever sat down," she said. "I think that's one of the special things about him. Even though he has the doctorate and the fancy credentials, he has a rapport with everybody in Idaho — the small cafe keepers, the miners, everyone. Nobody ever felt that because of his scholarship he was unapproachable."

At Boise's First Presbyterian Church, where the ailing Wells recently missed the Easter service for the first time in 69 years, Pastor Mark Davis called him "monumentally humble. He always sits at the back of the church in the balcony. I've known him 11 years and have never heard him use the first-person pronoun. It's always 'we.' Self isn't an issue with him. He's a man of non-self esteem. It isn't that he doesn't think well of himself. It's that he doesn't think about himself at all."

His novel twists on the first-person can be mixed, as in his response in a "Public Historian" article to being introduced at a national meeting of historians as the conscience of the preservation movement:

"I thought, well, this is at least something we've tried to be."

When Japanese Americans were interned at Minidoka during World War II, Wells, representing his church, was among the first to greet them and offer assistance.

"He's the goodest person I know," says Judy Austin, the historical society's coordinator of publications. "He's devoutly Christian. He doesn't wave banners about it. He just lives it."

Austin has chosen an inscription for her mentor's headstone.

"It's from Micah: 'What does the Lord require of thee but to do justice, love mercy and walk humbly with thy God?' That summarizes his whole life."

Wells's own summary is vintage Wells:

"I hope we accomplished something," he said when asked his greatest achievement. "We've been into so many different things it's hard to say one's more consequential than another. I'd like to be remembered for a variety of preservation and agency activities. But really, all I've done is what I've wanted to do. Historical research, preservation, development of the archives and agency libraries, these were all things I enjoyed doing. I never had someone telling me what to do.

"I did what I wanted and foisted the rest off onto someone else. The result was this great, long vacation."

Dr. Fuzzy
(Aug. 16, 2004)

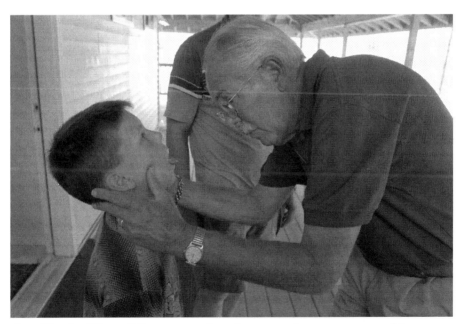

Dr. Charles "Fuzzy" Steuart performing a routine exam — on his front porch. His patient is Christopher Neu. (Gerry Melendez / Idaho Statesman)

ARCO — The first clue that Charles "Fuzzy" Steuart isn't your everyday doctor is a small sign on the fence outside his home office: a bull with a diagonal slash through it.

The second clue is his "waiting room," a cluster of plastic chairs around a patio table on his deck. Lying on the table are Steuart's cigarettes, coffee cup, portable phone and an ashtray with a smoldering butt.

Except for the deck and a hallway with a couple of chairs, there isn't a waiting room at the Skunk Mansion Clinic. It isn't needed because there are no long waits. Most patients are in and out in 10 minutes.

There's no receptionist, nurse or clerks. No medical charts, no appointments, no bills.

An office visit is $10. If you don't have ten bucks, he'll consider yard work, dog-sitting or a cold beer.

"I was a biochemist, I've done research, and I've run a traditional private practice," Arco's one-man clinic said. "It's all been fun. But now I'm doing it my way."

Steuart's may be the most unusual medical practice in Idaho. He has an examining room for procedures requiring privacy, but thinks nothing of examining patients on his deck with other patients providing a running commentary. His office is open four days a week, four hours a day. He refuses to work with insurance companies or the government, and, in heavily Mormon Arco, he sips coffee and smokes between patients.

No one seems to mind.

"I like him," said Helen Marinac, who drives 25 miles from Mackay to see Steuart. "He looks you in the eye and talks to you and treats you like a human being. My parents are in their 80s, and they love him. They don't have a lot of medical coverage and can get what they need here for $10. And medically, he's right on the money."

Steuart's $10 fee — he jokes that "one price fits all" — would be a bargain if he were an average doctor.

He isn't. The walls outside his examining room are lined with testimonials to medical achievement — Harvard (Phi Beta Kappa), Johns Hopkins University, medical certificates from Idaho, Oregon, Washington, Maryland and Florida. An internist and oncologist, he spent most of his career in Boise, where he was a founder of the Mountain States Tumor Institute.

"He's brilliant, abrasive and compassionate — in short, a Renaissance man," Boise physician David Weeks said. "When he practiced here, he was one of Boise's medical gurus."

A guru nicknamed "Fuzzy."

"When my mother was pregnant with me, they called me Buzzy," Steuart said. "Somehow that became Fuzzy. You know how doctors get stuffy and pompous when they start putting a lot of green in their pockets? I figured that if I kept a name like Fuzzy, I'd never get pompous."

Fuzzy moved to Arco, population 1,026, in September 2002. He was looking for a place where he could be semi-retired and practice medicine on his own terms. He wanted to live in a town where there was a hospital and at least one other doctor so he wouldn't always be on call. He wanted to be in an area where people were struggling financially and needed the services he had to offer. Arco, with a hospital, one other doctor and a sagging agricultural economy, seemed just about perfect. The passion of his wife, Kriss, for high-desert rockhounding sealed the deal.

Now 69, Steuart had spent his life practicing medicine on other people's terms. He'd had his fill of bureaucracies, regulations, paperwork, high overhead and administrative quagmires. He just wanted to be a doctor.

"There was one government insurance form that required 162 data entries, and if every one of them wasn't filled out, they wouldn't accept it," he said. "I decided I'd run a little practice where I didn't deal with government or insurance forms. I'd answer the phone myself, because when you call the doctor, the doctor is who you want to talk to.

"If you answer your own phone and don't make appointments, you don't need a receptionist. If you don't send out bills, you don't need a billing clerk. If the patients keep their own charts and you don't do any lab work in your office, you free yourself from all kinds of regulations.

I wanted to cut out all the extraneous stuff and do what a doctor is supposed to do, which is seeing patients."

Steuart has lab work done at the hospital. He refers patients who need it to hospitals or specialists. Patients at the Skunk Mansion Clinic sign in and pay when they arrive. The signature is the only paperwork.

Trevor Green still owes Steuart for taking care of a finger injured in an accident with a power saw. His follow-up visit resulted in a scene that could be considered typical at Skunk Mansion, but would occur almost nowhere else.

"Hi, Doc. I brought a beer for you," Green said, bounding onto the porch.

"There is a God," Steuart replied. "Uh-oh. Sadie, get back up here!"

Sadie is the Steuarts' black Lab.

"Oh, no! My wife is going to shoot me. Sadie, get back here!"

To everyone's surprise, Sadie runs back to the deck, down the hallway and into a bedroom, where she leaps onto a bed and watches the examination through an open window. Steuart continues as if nothing had happened. Green's fingernail is several shades of purple, but it's improving.

"Thank you, Dr. Fuzz," he says as he leaves, smiling broadly.

His payment, due when his finger heals: a song played on his guitar.

Exhibiting a gift for understatement, Green observed that "there aren't a lot of places that have a doctor like this. ... I heard about him from a friend and have really been impressed. This is how you get well, not dealing with the medical bureaucracy. Dr. Fuzz is good for the community."

Arco resident Freda Denny agreed.

"It's an unusual practice, but I like it. I had high blood pressure and a thyroid problem. Another doctor I went to didn't do anything to help me at all, but Dr. Steuart straightened me right out. A lot of doctors won't even let you see your medical chart, but he gives it to you. When you have your chart, you know exactly what's wrong with you. And $10 is a blessing for people like me on fixed incomes. Usually it's $58 or $60, and they don't know as much or do anything that makes you better."

Mary Ellen Romney says she "wouldn't go to anyone else. I like his personality and the way he treats people. ... I wish I had a dollar for every medical form I've signed. I don't have to do that here. I just bring him a six-pack of beer or whatever."

Steuart has come a long way to get to his unconventional clinic in Arco. He grew up in Maryland and in college seriously considered majoring in literature.

"I was in my junior year when I decided I didn't want to spend my lifetime digging out metaphors in James Joyce. So I got out the medical applications and went to Hopkins."

After graduating from Johns Hopkins, he taught two years at the University of Miami, where he learned through a friend of an opportunity in Boise at what eventually became MSTI.

"I came out here to do cancer research and have been here ever since," he said. "Idaho's the only place I've been that I wanted to come back to."

Though he's been in Arco only two years, he feels at home there. Between the clinic and his wife's job as a home health nurse, they know just about everyone in town.

"In Boise, I knew one of my neighbors, " he said. "Here, I know them all."

Besides running the clinic, he's an occasional substitute teacher at the high school.

"I teach biology, science, chemistry, English, P.E, whatever they need. I enjoy the kids, and I can give back as good as they can shell out."

He sees five to 15 patients a day. Even at 15 a day, and assuming they didn't pay in beer, he makes a fraction of what he could with a conventional practice in a bigger city.

That doesn't seem to faze him.

"The only decent-paying jobs in Arco are at the school and the hospital, " he said. "People here are poor. They needed someone like me."

A Regular Gal
(May 30, 2010)

Occasionally — not often, because there aren't a lot of them in Idaho — readers ask what it's like for reporters to meet famous people.

The answer depends on the famous person. A few are world-class jerks, but most are just regular people who happen to be famous.

Regular people are my stock-in-trade as story subjects. I like them and am comfortable with them. That's why, on the night I had dinner with Lynn Redgrave, the famous actress, I was looking for a regular person to talk to instead.

I'm sorry this is late. My intention was to write it shortly after her death, on May 2, but other stories got in the way.

So how does an obscure Idaho columnist end up having dinner with a world-famous celebrity?

By sheerest accident.

The occasion was the 10th anniversary of the Morrison Center. Velma Morrison was hosting a $250 a plate dinner at her home, and The Statesman paid $250 for me to go and write about it.

For someone whose idea of dressing up is jeans without holes in them, it was unnerving. Some of the men were dressed in tuxedos. Most of those who weren't were wearing suits that cost more than my car. The women were wearing gowns and expensive jewelry. No jeans anywhere.

The guest list included corporation presidents, university presidents, congressmen, society mavens, a governor or two … You could have thrown a boomerang and not hit anyone who had been inside a tavern, trailer park or bowling alley.

I was looking for someone I'd feel comfortable having dinner with and not finding anyone when my attention was drawn to a regular-looking guy in a string tie, sitting alone at a table for 12.

Figuring that he was as uncomfortable as I was, I pulled up a chair beside him.

And that's how I met the world-famous raptor expert, Morley Nelson.

"Anyone sitting here?" I asked him.

"I don't think so."

I thought he was joking until a big shot asked if he and his wife could join us.

"No. Lynn and her family are sitting here."

Lynn was Redgrave, who was appearing at the Morrison Center that evening in a one-woman play she'd written. Searching for regular folks, I had stumbled into the last seat at the VIP table.

You can imagine my reaction when Redgrave herself sat down beside me, so close our elbows were touching, and introduced herself.

As if she needed an introduction. This was a member of one of Britain's preeminent acting families — Sir Michael Redgrave, Vanessa Redgrave and Natasha Richardson, to name a few. She'd become a household word in the title role of "Georgy Girl," was nominated for two Oscars and was critically acclaimed on both stage and screen.

As if that weren't enough, she was then omnipresent on television in a series of Weight Watchers commercials. I might as well have been sitting next to Oprah.

Normally, the situation would have left me tongue-tied.

It probably did, in fact, until I realized something startling. I was sitting between two of the most regular people in the room.

Redgrave couldn't have been nicer. In the unlikely event that you didn't know who she was, you'd never have guessed that she was a star. It wasn't just that she was utterly lacking in attitude; she had a way of effortlessly putting you at ease. It was like talking to an old friend over a beer. She was funny and genuinely interested in what you had to say, even if she'd heard it before. In two minutes, you felt as if you'd known her for years.

Nelson, as anyone who knew him can attest, was cut from the same cloth. No one was more down to earth. We talked about acting, birds, population control... I've never enjoyed an evening more.

It's hard to believe they're both gone now: two people who made it to the top of their chosen professions, received worldwide acclaim and had the good sense not to let it go to their heads.

I've been missing Morley, who later became a friend, for years. Now I miss both of my onetime dinner companions.

Landing at their table was one of the luckiest accidents of my life.

The $250 lasagna wasn't bad, either.

Morley
(April 24, 1994)

Morley Nelson paces the front room of his Foothills home, six-shooter in hand, eyes blazing at the memory of someone daring to shoot at his eagles.

"People would shoot at my birds, so I'd put one (a bullet) in the ditch beside them," he says, checking the chamber to make sure he doesn't put one through his living-room wall. "It almost started some gun battles."

That was before Idaho's one-man raptor show changed the popular image of birds of prey as birds to be preyed upon.

One of the nation's foremost raptor experts, Nelson led the battle to create Idaho's Snake River Birds of Prey Natural Area. He has helped bring back species from the edge of extinction and helped bring Idaho the World Center for Birds of Prey, now celebrating its 10th anniversary.

He successfully lobbied for protected-species legislation for golden and bald eagles and has worked with celebrities from Walt Disney to Robert Redford on films telling the great birds' story.

"Morley is internationally known for his films and his advocacy in protecting the Snake River Birds of Prey Area," says Tom Cade, founding chairman of the Peregrine Fund. "Everywhere I go around the world, his name crops up. Everyone knows about Morley."

At 77, Nelson does 40 pushups every morning. Tough and straight-talking, he is a battle-scarred veteran of dissimilar wars. He won a bronze star, silver star and purple heart in World War II. A bridge fills a gap left by a tooth lost while playing professional hockey. A scar from an eagle talon traces a line across his forehead.

"Listen," he says as a series of hooting calls rises from the brushy hillside behind his North Boise home. "The eagles are whistling. They're saying hello to me."

Nelson "speaks" Eagle. He says he knows when his birds are saying, among other things, "come here," "go away," "I want food," "be careful," and "let's breed."

"That's what she's saying," he says, pointing to a tethered prairie falcon. "She wants to set up housekeeping."

Empty nesters, Nelson and wife, Pat, share a life beguiled by birds. Bird paintings and bird figurines decorate their living room. The hill rising from the swimming pool behind their home is dotted with pens, perches and sheds for birds from common hawks to "Pearl," the magnificent bald eagle used for U.S. Postal Service logos. Nelson talks continuously as he climbs the slope, weaving a seamless dialogue with birds and visitors.

"I don't use the pool, but I swim with my dog in the river every day. Come here, big hawk. ... Did you hear that? She said 'OK.' If it wasn't, she'd take you by the nose and put you out of your misery."

With a gloved hand, he picks up an enormous golden eagle.

"This glove's too thin. That's a big mistake. ... All right, big hawk. You can go back now. You're a good hawk."

Nelson warns guests that handling the birds is more difficult and dangerous than he makes it look.

"You have to know them, or you're going to wear some awful scars."

Nelson's affair with birds of prey began on his parents' ranch in North Dakota. Ten at the time, he was riding his horse when his dog scared up a flock of teal. The boy watched as a falcon flying more than 100 mph struck one of the teal.

"I'd never seen anything like that. I didn't know there was anything that fast."

He trained his first hawk when he was 12.

"The thing that got me in the beginning was the grace and beauty, the nobility of these birds. If you wound an eagle, he'll still come at you. They'll fight to the death, and if they like you they'll defend you to the death. That's why so many countries have chosen them as their emblems."

Nelson's interest in raptors continued through high school and his years at North Dakota State University, where he majored in soil science and engineering. The day after the Japanese bombed Pearl Harbor, he joined the army.

The army found his college education useful in establishing desert training centers. His boss was Gen. George Patton, one of the war's most colorful (and volatile) figures. Patton was furious when he saw Nelson wearing the six-shooter he still keeps in his Boise home.

"He said only generals could wear nonregulation firearms. He wanted to take away my gun and my stripes."

When the general calmed down, Nelson bet him he could shoot a perfect score on the firing range using his six-shooter at twice the distance specified for regulation firearms.

He won the bet.

"I didn't respect Patton," he recalled. "I cared about the soil and the water and the people. All he cared about was the military."

After the war, Nelson worked as a soils scientist in the Southwest and Utah. His life changed the first time he saw the Snake River Canyon.

"I was amazed at what a magnificent place it was," he said. "Nowhere in the world had anybody recorded eagles and falcons like that."

In 1948, he moved to Boise as head of the Columbia River Basin Snow Survey and Water Supply Forecast. His work put him in frequent contact with raptors, which he studied, filmed and wrote about on his own time. A national reputation followed.

Magazines from "Life" to "Smithsonian" published articles about him. Working with Disney, he helped dispel the image of raptors as dangerous killers.

"People thought eagles were killing babies and carrying off sheep."

One Disney film, "Ida the Offbeat Eagle," was shot in the Snake River Canyon using an eagle as the story's hero.

"A total of 420 million people ended up seeing the canyon through those films," Nelson said. "The power of that many people seeing it was what got Congress to go along with the birds of prey area."

"The Eagle and the Hawk," made with Paul Newman and Joanne Woodward's daughter Nell Newman, showed a hawk trying to land after being shot. The scene touched even those who previously killed the birds.

Nelson is among the first to know of a wounded bird. He has been finding ways to prevent or ease their suffering for years.

In the '70s, he invented a device that has saved untold numbers of eagles. The birds were being electrocuted when their wings touched wires during attempted landings on power poles. By studying landings of a trained eagle on model poles, he devised a safe landing platform. Today, his invention is used on power towers around the world.

Early this year, he saved several hawks close to death after eating poisoned starlings.

Not all of his stories have happy endings. About 20 percent of the birds he treats are too far gone to survive.

One of the current patients at his hillside home will never fly again. A shooting victim, it has only one wing.

Although he can't save all of the birds he loves, he has done more to assure their continued survival than anyone knows. In 1952, Nelson predicted that artificial insemination and incubators could be used to increase birds-of-prey populations. Many scoffed at the idea, now standard procedure at the world center he helped bring to Idaho.

One of the most dramatic success stories is that of the peregrine falcon, once all but exterminated by chemical poisoning. In the late '60s, the peregrine was extinct east of the Mississippi. In the West, its numbers had been reduced by 90 percent.

Today, the peregrine is making a comeback throughout its range. The Peregrine Fund has released an estimated 4,000 birds in the wild. About half were bred at the world center. The center also is home to 12 of the world's 70 remaining California condors.

Success breeds opportunity, but the man who talks to eagles is content with what he has.

"I've been offered jobs by Disney and jobs in Washington, D.C., but this is where the wind and the cliffs and the birds are. This is where I'll always be."

The Three Lives of Joe Munch
(Feb. 1, 2009)

Legendary tough guy Joe Munch was reflecting on the forces that have shaped his life when he did something his critics would say was wildly out of character.

The former child Nazi, French Legionnaire, cop and chief of security at Idaho's penitentiary — dry-eyed through the carnage of war and the harshness of prison life — paused and wiped away a tear.

"You ask me which is the real Joe Munch," he said. "It's all of them. I've been the person who fit the situation."

On a table beside the lounge chair where he now spends much of his time was a box of memorabilia from his years in the French Foreign Legion. Next to that, his Hitler Youth knife — its Blut und Ehre (Blood and Honor) inscription still eerily sinister.

Munch was resting after a blood transfusion for the esophageal cancer that could end his life at any time. Even dressed in slippers, baggy pants and an Ada County Sheriff's Employees Association T-shirt, he evokes images of the hard-boiled soldier and cop he once was — commanding presence, neatly trimmed gray hair swept straight back, gray-blue eyes that could cut steel.

At 77, Munch still carries his draft card. On his front lawn, American and Idaho flags ripple from a tall pole. More than flags, they're testimonials to the onetime Nazi's feelings for a country he once saw as an enemy but for most of his life has been fiercely proud to call home.

"This is the most wonderful country in the world," he said, his German accent undiluted by almost half a century here. "I wouldn't give up my citizenship if you cut my hand off."

How he got here and his life since is a story unique in Idaho lore.

"Every once in a while I get sentimental and cry, talking about the good and bad things in my life," he said. "I think there's been more good than bad."

Mike Johnson's first glimpse of Joe Munch created a lifelong impression.

It was 1972, the year of the big riot at the old Idaho Penitentiary on Warm Springs Avenue. A former U.S. Marshal and Boise airport police chief, Johnson was then a rookie emergency medical technician.

"Suddenly here came this guy who was larger than life," he said. "He came out of the big steel doors at the pen with an inmate under each arm. There were flames 100 feet high, and here came Superman."

Munch was the penitentiary's chief of security, a job for which he was uniquely suited. His apprenticeship began in Nazi Germany, where he was imprisoned at 15, and in the French Foreign Legion, in which he was serving when the French government jailed him for joining a rebellion against President Charles de Gaulle. He also was imprisoned in Vietnam. Prison was to Munch what college is for luckier students.

Boise City Councilman Vern Bisterfeldt, a former police officer who worked with him, describes Munch as having had "enough life for three lifetimes."

The first began with his birth, in Bergheim-Erft, Germany, in 1931. He joined the paramilitary Hitler Youth organization as a young boy; service was all but compulsory. His father served on the Russian Front; his mother welded Panzer and Tiger tanks. By the war's end, the family was living in Duren, where 14-year-old Josef delivered ammunition to Nazi anti-aircraft gunners.

"We got bombed by the Americans and lost everything," he said. "I hated Americans. I was taught that they were all bullies and gangsters."

With his father presumed to have died in the battle of Stalingrad and his mother working at a post-war Allied headquarters and dating one of the hated Americans there, he rebelled by running away. Arrested for stealing sausage, he spent six months in prison and escaped by jumping onto a potato truck.

Desperate but still rebellious, he made his way to a French-operated jail, lied about his age and joined the French Foreign Legion. His first life was over, the second just beginning.

"I disappeared in the French Foreign Legion for 14 years. It was the only military outfit that would take Germans."

Just 16 but already battle-hardened in the near annihilation of Hitler's Germany, Munch proved to be an apt soldier. He completed paratrooper training and made more than 100 jumps, serving in Vietnam, Laos, the Congo, Kenya, Somalia, Tunisia, Morocco and Algiers. He learned combat skills and became proficient in the use of explosives.

"I loved to blow things up."

When he joined the French Foreign Legion, Munch was an angry, street-smart boy. When he left, he was a combat machine. He witnessed history, did things no one should ever have to do. His years as a soldier helped shape him into what former Ada County sheriff's detective Mike Roberts called "a command force. You could look at him clear across a room and tell that this was one guy you shouldn't mess with.

"In his prime, he had the coldest, steel-gray eyes I ever saw. You knew there was something behind those eyes. He wasn't afraid of God Himself."

Munch spent most of his years as a Legionnaire in Indochina, primarily Vietnam, fighting Communists. He spent a year and a half as a prisoner of war in Vietnam, where he said his teeth were knocked out and he was whipped daily.

In 1952, his outfit was ordered to blow up a church in Laos.

There were 200 to 300 people — men, women and children — in that church," he said. "After we blew it up, American pilots napalmed it. At the time, I didn't feel anything."

In Algeria, he was among the Legionnaires who joined the Organization of the Secret Army, made famous in the book and film, "Day of the Jackal." The O.A.S. revolted against de Gaulle for his support of Algerian independence from France.

"We took the city of Algiers and held it until de Gaulle sent in his regulars. I was a legion officer by then. The officers were sent to a military prison in Constantine for treason. I was there nine months. I saw them execute officers. When my turn came, they said I could be executed or join a disciplinary company in the Sahara Desert. Which would you choose?"

The disciplinary unit, which included men convicted of violent crimes, was considered the most dangerous duty the legion had to offer. Munch slept with a machine gun.

"At this point I was working for de Gaulle's side," he said. "We were fighting rebels who were fighting him. Every week we rounded them up, made them dig their own graves, then 'bing, bing, bing.'

"If I did that now, I'd be hanging on a gallows. I'd do it differently now. But with the information I had then, I did what I had to do. Life didn't mean anything to me then."

That was about to change.

On leave from the legion in 1962, Munch came to the U.S. to visit his mother. She'd married the American she'd met at Allied headquarters and was living in Idaho. Her son didn't realize it at the time, but he was coming home.

"I didn't want to go to the U.S.," he said. "In the legion we got free wine, beer and cigarettes. But when I visited my mother in Payette, everybody was friendly. There were so many women I didn't know what to do with them. And I'd always wanted to get married."

He married Shirley Crosby of Payette, a former Army stenographer who recalled that he was "good-looking and had a cute butt." She "was 29 and desperate."

He fought forest fires and operated heavy equipment, but the job that changed his life was working as a tower guard at the old penitentiary. It paid $175 a month. When a prisoner decided to test the new guard by sitting on a bucket in defiance of an order, Munch shot the bucket out from under him.

"I was never afraid of inmates," he said. "I knew about prison. I was always a step ahead of them."

He advanced quickly, rising to lieutenant, captain and chief of security. He also taught at the police academy and at sheriffs' departments.

When prisoners dug tunnels, he monitored their progress and greeted the escapees with tear gas. He personally retrieved every inmate who escaped on his watch.

His punishments included restricting inmates to baby food for up to six months. An inmate who stole 24 eggs was forced to eat them. Munch's standing order to guards who witnessed escape attempts: shoot to kill.

When three prisoners held a knife to a guard's throat, Munch fired a machine gun at them.

They dropped the knife.

Prisoners weren't his only targets. In 1977, he blew the whistle on what he judged to be a corrupt prison administration. It cost him his job, but he was vindicated when a governor's panel asked the warden and director of corrections to resign.

Working at the prison was his favorite job "because of the results I could see later. Inmates everyone said would never make it rejoined society. Some own their own businesses now."

In 1979, the Ada County Sheriff's Department hired the ex-prison boss as a deputy.

"He had absolutely no tolerance for drunk drivers," Sheriff Gary Raney said. "He was gruff and not politically correct, but everyone respected him. He was rarely involved in the use of force. I'd describe him as a guy who was caring on the inside, but had to toughen up on the outside because of all he'd been through early in his life."

In some ways, the tough guy remains defiantly unapologetic: Prisoners like harsh discipline; Idaho's new penitentiary is "a kindergarten." The O.A.S. was right. Waterboarding is OK.

"Politically correct isn't in his dictionary," Johnson said.

In other ways, according to Shirley Munch, her husband is "a teddy bear."

In fact, a teddy bear dressed in a deputy's uniform lent the appearance of a partner on his night patrols. Munch retired from the department in 1998, after serving 19 years and placing more than 100 crosses at sites of fatal accidents.

At the prison, he and his wife organized Easter Egg hunts for inmates and their children.

As a boy, he wanted to be a Catholic priest.

"After I came to this country, I felt sorry about the people I'd killed," he said. "I confessed and talked to two priests about it. They said I'd be forgiven."

In December, sheriff's department employees held a blood drive to help with Munch's transfusions. People from as far away as Gooding participated.

His prognosis remains day to day.

"When I think of all I've been through, I've been lucky," he said. "I don't want to die, but if it's my time, I'm ready. I'm not afraid of it."

Editor's note: Joe Munch died March 1, 2009.

Old West Lawman
(Jan. 31, 2010)

A brand inspector for 28 years, Lynn Gibson has worked with cattle since he was a kid. (Darin Oswald / Idaho Statesman)

INDIAN VALLEY — Where a city person sees a herd of generic cattle, Lynn Gibson sees breeds, brands, earmarks and tags identifying each cow and its owner.

Ownership has become an issue in the 2,800 square miles he roams as an Idaho brand inspector. Cattle rustling, a crime usually associated with the Old West, is alive and well there.

A mirror of hard times, rustling is thought to be responsible for the disappearance of more than 2,000 cows in Oregon, Nevada and Idaho since 2007. Other neighboring states have reported smaller losses.

In Idaho, the hot spot is the Indian Valley area, part of Gibson's two-county territory. Rustlers are suspected of stealing more than 300 cows worth more than $250,000 there in two years.

"It's almost impossible to catch them at it," he says. "It's not like a busted window. Somebody breaks your window, you know it. You don't have to break a window to steal a cow. It can be plumb out of the country before you even know it's missing."

Idaho is one of 12 states that employ brand inspectors like Gibson, who ensure that brands are legally registered and the animals bearing them are in the possession of their registered owners. All 12 are in the West.

"They can get away without inspectors back East, where cattle are confined," he said. "In a state as wide open as Idaho, with cattle turned out to range, you'd be lucky to get any cows back if you didn't have brand inspectors."

Normally, his job is to inspect cattle when they leave the state, change owners or are slaughtered. Lately, he's been working day and night to solve the most vexing case of his career — how cattle are vanishing like mist from an area he knows the way most people know their backyards.

"Cows disappear for lots of reasons," he said. "Lightning, poisonous weeds, wolves. Ranchers have an idea how many they should lose to natural causes. If the numbers are beyond that, there has to be a reason."

"You can't blame it all on predators," State Brand Inspector Larry Hayhurst added. "Some of it's two-legged predators."

Midvale rancher Steve Sutton is one of some 30 ranchers who have lost cattle. He lost 12 bred (pregnant) cows, six calves and a bull last year, worth $17,000.

"That's three times my normal loss," he said. "I can't sustain that. And you don't know who's doing it unless you catch them red-handed."

Even then, the suspects can claim it was an honest mistake and have a chance of getting away with it.

"How do you prove your calf didn't just go through a hole in a fence onto the wrong property?" Gibson said. "You probably can't."

You might not even be able to prove it's your calf. Brands can be altered. A brand on a hip means a different owner than the same brand on a shoulder. Brands are added whenever animals are sold, and just seeing brands can be difficult.

"That's a lick mark," Gibson said to a chagrined reporter who thought he'd spotted one. "Cows licking each other. It can be tough to see brands with the cows all haired up for winter."

He knows ranchers as well as their cattle, saying with a straight face that he inspects "people as much as cows. I know who needs watching and who doesn't."

Ranchers say he's the right man for the job.

"I've known him all my life," Sutton said. "Once he's on a deal like this, he doesn't stop."

Gibson, 58, has been a brand inspector 27 years. He grew up on a ranch at Crane Creek Reservoir, now part of his territory, and went on his first cattle drive at 11. At 15, he had his own truck and worked for neighbors, making sure their cows were fed, healthy and where they belonged. In one way or another, he's been inspecting cattle most of his life.

He and his wife own an elk ranch near Weiser, and he looks like the rancher he is — worn boots and jeans, drooping mustache, sweat-stained ball cap. He patrols a brain-boggling network of back roads in a 2001 Chevrolet pickup packed with police radios, a spotting scope, range finder, binoculars, a Howa .231 rifle and an Idaho brand book with information on more than 2,700 brands. A .45 with elk-antler grips hangs from his belt.

"There have been a couple of times when I've had my shotgun out from under my duster, but thank God, I haven't had to use it," he said. "I'd hate to have to start doing that, but I like just about everything else about this job. How many people get to spend their life doing what they love in a setting like this?"

The setting was an alpine valley glittering with snow. Gibson knows every ranch, every rancher there.

"I respect these guys. They're feeding this country. They're out there working hard every day in the mud and the blood and the beer. I went to school with some of them. To me, this is personal.

"Whoever's doing this has gotta be somebody that's in the community and knows cows. If they didn't, I'd catch them in a minute. It's neighbor taking from neighbor. Somebody trying to make a quick buck."

He thinks most of the cattle are being taken when they're on summer range deep in the mountains.

"Ranchers are pretty trusting. They'll put a $1,200 cow out where people can take it. Would you put a $1,200 TV out on the street in Boise?"

Thieves could move the cows in horse trailers, common sights locally, and their owners wouldn't know they were missing until they failed to return from the range in the fall or winter.

"We don't drive around looking for them to steal a cow," Gibson said. "You could drive around till hell freezes over and not see anything. That's why we did the saturation patrol."

The saturation patrol was this fall, when Gibson worked 45 days without a day off. He and an assistant patrolled U.S. 95 night and day, watching for unfamiliar vehicles hauling cattle and stopping trucks to check brands. They found nothing they could prove was illegal.

"You have to prove intent. If a toolbox is in the back of the wrong pickup, it's pretty obvious it was stolen. But cows get shuffled around."

"These rustlers we're dealing with now aren't stupid," Gibson said. "If they were, they'd be caught by now."

"They've got a system," Hayhurst said, "a mechanism that's getting cows past our system."

Gibson figures the rustlers are disposing of the cows in one of three ways. One is to "put their own irons (brands) on them, mix them with their own herds, and keep them for a couple of years before selling them. We'd know they were in the cow business, so it wouldn't raise many red flags. If it was somebody who said they just bought a cow from a local rancher, we'd ask to see the brand inspection."

Another way, he said, would be to "shuffle them onto a feedlot, get them branded with the feedlot iron and pass them off to an Oregon inspector. He wouldn't know the cows that are missing in our area.

"Or they're getting them clear out of the country to someplace like Nebraska. They don't have brand laws there." (Part of Nebraska is a brand area; the rest isn't.)

The cows represent a 3 to 5 percent loss of stock for local ranches. Loss to natural causes normally is 1 percent. The thefts are serious enough — they could put small ranchers out of business — that for the last nine months Gibson has been getting help from the U.S. Forest Service, three counties, the Idaho State Police and three state departments.

"We need more eyes, more surveillance, more people looking at paperwork," Hayhurst said.

Adding to the challenge for law enforcement officers is a legal system that makes convictions and sentencing problematic. Unlike the Old West, where rustlers were hanged, the New West tends to view them as curiosities.

"I've seen people get five years, 10 years, but not often," Hayhurst said. "It's hard to get overworked prosecutors to even take the cases. Most judges aren't interested, and juries don't even know how the game is played. They think all the beef comes from Albertsons."

That said, he adds that "Lynn will never sleep until this is solved."

On call 24/7, Gibson could have retired two years ago but wants to "stick around until we get this handled. I think we can do that, especially now that we've got some outside help. But it's still hard. It's not like having a cow taken out of your backyard. This is a pretty big backyard."

Salmon River Caveman
(Oct. 24, 1993)

ELK BEND — When Dugout Dick Zimmerman began building his unusual home overlooking the Salmon River, all he wanted was a cave where he could be away from people. He never dreamed it would attract them.

What began in 1948 with a trickle of curious motorists has become a stream of river runners and other visitors.

Growth is good for business — on a good day, he makes $12 from river floaters who tour his caves but he worries that he's losing his privacy.

"I have neighbors across the river now, " he grumps. "...I can't even stand outside to take a leak anymore."

The home of the "Salmon River caveman," 19 miles south of the town of Salmon, is one of Idaho's stranger sights. Some 20 caves line the rocky mountainside overlooking the river. Some are used for storage, but 10 are habitable and intermittently rented.

The slope is dotted with cow skulls, old tires, ancient refrigerators and other junk. Plumes of smoke curl from rusty pipes rising from the rock. Seen from across the river on U.S. 93, it looks like a Flintstones cartoon come to life.

Zimmerman dug the caves alone, using only a pick, a shovel and a pry bar. He was 32 when he came to the canyon. Now 77, he has been living in a cave for 45 years.

"I don't know why I dug so many," he says. "I guess it was just to be doing something, and the rocks were here. I never meant to build an apartment house."

The biggest caves are some 60 feet deep, with rooms up to 15 feet wide. One has a sun porch, enclosed with windshields from old cars. Most have an old refrigerator or two, for storage.

A few are more like rock houses than caves. Tires anchored in soil keep his six goats from digging beds in their sod roofs. Depending on size and amenities, he rents the "apartments" for $10, $15 or $25 a month.

Social Security, rent from his tenants and fees from tours he gives to river floaters average about $200 a month, all the income he needs. His expenses are minimal — no mortgage, no electricity or telephone, no monthly bills. The land belongs to the Bureau of Land Management, but mining claims allow him to live there rent-free the rest of his life.

"I have everything here," he says. "I got lots of rocks and rubber tires. I have plenty of straw and fruit and vegetables, my dog and my cats and my guitars. I make wine to cook with. There's nothing I really need."

As the number of caves and the extent of his reputation grew, the man who wanted only to be left alone found himself a local celebrity.

People passing on the highway see the caves and stop to ask about them. Reporters ask for interviews. Television crews stop to photograph him. In December, Zimmerman was featured in National Geographic magazine. He has turned down offers to appear as a guest on the "Tonight" show.

"I told them I didn't want to go to California and that I ride Greyhounds, not airplanes," he said. "Besides, the show isn't in California. The show is here."

The "show" has become the source of a modest, seasonal income for him. A pragmatic hermit, he now welcomes summer visitors, who pay a dollar apiece to tour his caves, take pictures and hear folk music from a gone era.

"Would you like to hear something?" he asks, strapping on a beat-up guitar.

Something turns out to be "Wreck of the '97," a hobo song. He taps his feet and sings, pounds chords on his guitar, blows into a harmonica. It's awful, but somehow appealing. With his gravel wail, weathered face and wispy, white hair, he could be Bob Dylan's grandfather.

For a cave, his home is surprisingly comfortable. An estimated 12 feet wide by 30 deep, it has a woodstove and lanterns, a table and chairs, a wooden bed with a mattress, a tube that brings drinking water from a spring in the rocks. Bathing is done in a metal washtub, or, in summer, the river.

A wooden door and wood-framed windows wedged into the entrance let in light and keep out cold. The rock holds heat for days. He says he uses half a cord of wood per winter. Last winter, he returned from visiting his family, cousins in the Midwest, to find the temperature inside the cave had changed little from when he left. Outside, it had reached 40 below.

In a typical month, three or four of the caves are occupied. In the fall, some of his renters are hunters, who pay $2 a night. The rest he kindly describes as "guys that don't have much money. They're kind of down and out when they come here."

Dugout Dick spent his childhood in Indiana fascinated by caves.

"I've liked caves as long as I can remember," he says. "When I was little, I used to go down to the Yellow River and make little dugouts. I liked to play in them. It was cool and quiet there. I liked that."

The dugouts were more than cool and quiet. They were an escape from the world of people. Zimmerman was born in 1916 and grew up poor. The oldest of five children, he was unpopular in school, unhappy at home.

"I never did get along with my Dad," he recalls. "He was ornery and mean. A bootlegger."

Fights at school were common. Victories weren't.

"I was kind of backward and shy as a kid. I got picked on quite a bit. I was a farm boy and didn't know how to protect myself. I wouldn't fight, so they'd pick on me."

In his teens, he worked as a farm laborer. The work was hard, the pay low. When he was 19, his last tie to Indiana was broken.

"I had a girl leave me. She wanted a man who played basketball. That's when I decided to leave."

He hopped a westbound freight, worked two years on a ranch in Nebraska and hitchhiked to Idaho. After serving as an army truck driver during World War II, he returned to Idaho and spent three years herding sheep and lambs. By then the thing he craved most was independence — a home, a garden, a place to be away from people who picked on one another. The Salmon River canyon was ideal.

Asked why he never married, he gives an unexpected answer:

"I'm married now! I have a Mexican wife, but I haven't seen her in 15 years. She's welcome to come back if she wants. She knows where I'm at."

He says his wife left him because of his diet, which he admits is a little strange. Unable to eat meat, wheat or sugar because they upset his stomach, he lives primarily on fresh vegetables, dried fruits, homemade yogurt flavored with carrots and onions, and mush made with rye flour, stinging nettles, goat's milk and fermented vegetables.

"People think I'm crazy because of the way I eat," he says.

At 77, he craves little. In summer, he spends most of his time working in his one-acre garden and orchard. The land is irrigated with a windmill he designed and built to draw water from the river. A prospector of sorts, he has found enough copper to justify his mining claims, but enjoys renting and exhibiting his caves more than mining them.

In the winter, he holes up in his cave. If he gets bored, he reads magazines or his Bible (he can and does quote lengthy sections of scripture to anyone who will listen), goes for a walk with his dog, Eddy, or drives to Salmon in his battered pickup.

"I don't know many people there, but they know me. People I don't know smile and wave. I guess I'm kind of a local character. It's because the way I live is a little different. ... I don't get bored often. I've lived so much this way I don't know anything else."

He wouldn't live in a real house if he could.

"When I go away, I miss it," he says of his cave. "It's warm in winter, cool in summer. I'm as comfortable or more comfortable than I'd be in a house. I've stayed in houses. I don't like them."

Some people would look down on a person who lives in a cave. Dugout Dick Zimmerman looks down on his canyon and his river, his retreat from society, without regrets. He is a man content with the unusual life he has chosen.

"A cousin from Indiana came here once," he said with more than a trace of pride. "He thought I was poor and didn't have nothin' and that I'd better come and live right.

"When he saw all this, he changed his mind."

Editor's note: Dugout Dick Zimmerman died April 21, 2010. He was 94.

No One Laughed When Mr. Morrison Left
(Feb. 5, 1995)

No one celebrated when Harry Morrison left.

When word came that William Agee was retiring as chief executive officer of Morrison Knudsen Corp., employees honked horns in the company parking lot. They partied at Buster's, all but did cartwheels in the hallways.

This was not damning with faint praise. It was damning with resounding joy, which is infinitely worse.

I didn't know Bill Agee. But I knew Harry Morrison, the company's co-founder, and the difference between them couldn't be greater.

In Agee's defense, it can be said that few executives wouldn't suffer by comparison. They don't make leaders like Mr. Morrison anymore.

The "Mr." is intentional. Even people who worked with him for years addressed him as Mr. Morrison. He commanded that kind of respect.

Lyman Wilbur, the company's chief engineer for more than 20 years, says people were willing to work for MK for less than they could make elsewhere because they considered it a privilege to work with the man. He was a figure of enormous authority, but he didn't make employees feel small. He trusted their judgment, helped them with personal problems, loaned them money when times were hard.

This was a man honored on the cover of Time as having "done more than anyone else to change the face of the Earth." A giant. Yet he never lost the ability to empathize with those who weren't.

You wouldn't have caught Harry Morrison schmoozing at Pebble Beach while devoted employees were getting axed back home.

I knew him through his stepson. Velma Morrison's oldest son and I were in a band together in high school, and we practiced at the Morrisons' home on Harrison Boulevard. It was a nice home, but not pretentious. Its owner didn't need to show off. His accomplishments were more than enough.

I'll never forget my introduction to the famous Mr. Morrison. He was looking out the window of his darkened living room, watching the traffic on Harrison, undoubtedly thinking big thoughts. White hair, craggy face, furrowed brow. It was like being introduced to God.

I was 16 and terrified. Then he shook my hand, made a good-humored remark about our music, and suddenly I could breathe again. God was a regular guy.

He was getting on by then, nearly 80, and in failing health. Why he put up with us is a mystery. He couldn't have liked our whanging away week after week, but he remained cordial, even encouraging.

"Play well, boys," he would say. "Do your best."

"We will, Mr. Morrison."

And we did. To do less would have been sacrilegious.

He was so distinguished looking. Even though he was ill, not going anywhere or expecting anyone, he always looked imposing – impeccably dressed, often in a dark suit with a tie, his bearing erect, his presence majestic. I remember thinking he would have made a good president.

I don't remember thinking anything remotely like that about Bill Agee, or, for that matter, Bill Clinton.

There was something rock-solid about leaders like Harry Morrison. They had survived wars, weathered the Depression, gone from having nothing to changing the face of the Earth.

When they said things would be all right, you believed them.

When time proved it, that was when you celebrated.

When they were gone, you mourned.

That was the difference.

Mr. Spud
(May 26, 2008)

J.R. Simplot in December 1998. (Kim Hughes / Idaho Statesman)

The richest man in Idaho used to celebrate Halloween by handing silver dollars to the trick-or-treaters who trudged to his hilltop home. Each dollar came with an admonition to "make it grow," words that embodied J.R. Simplot's long and prosperous life.

John Richard Simplot, who died Sunday at 99, was one of the last of the old-time entrepreneurs, a farm boy who never went to high school but built a personal fortune Forbes magazine last estimated at $3.6 billion in 2007. The company he began with the flip of a coin grew into one of the largest agribusiness conglomerates in the world.

He was agricultural Idaho's only billionaire and a high-tech tycoon of the New West. Simplot's wealth allowed him to bankroll the start-up of Micron Technology Inc. He and other principals helped chart the future of what is now the state's largest private employer at board meetings held in a Boise pancake house.

"His legacy is his vision," said Gov. Butch Otter, Simplot's former son-in-law. "Compared with him, the rest of the world was wearing bifocals."

His credo: Work hard, hire good people and trust them to work hard.

Simplot claimed to own more deeded land than any other man in America. He owned the nation's largest cattle ranch in Oregon and had holdings from China to Chile. But nowhere was his influence more dominant than in Idaho, where he funded scores of business and educational and charitable enterprises. He donated millions to the state's colleges and universities and funded causes from Boise's Basque Museum to the Pocatello Public Library. He was recognized last week as a founding donor of the Idaho Community Foundation. His business interests were ubiquitous, covering the spectrum from Micron and the Idaho Steelheads to obscure but potentially profitable inventors and tinkerers.

Almost 30,000 people work for companies Simplot founded or financed. As of 2006, the J.R. Simplot Co. had 3,500 Idaho employees and about 10,000 worldwide. And some 9,000 Micron workers in the Treasure Valley alone owe their high-tech jobs in part to the man more responsible than anyone for the state's instantaneous identification with the humble spud.

Earthy, plainspoken, often profane, Simplot was to the potato what Henry Ford was to the automobile. He and his company improved the quality of potatoes, all but invented frozen french fries and dehydrated potatoes, and put "Famous Potatoes" on the map and the state's license plates. He supplied billions of fries for billions of fast-food customers, and in his 90s remained a fixture on the streets of Boise, larger than life in his Lincoln Town Car with the "Mr. Spud" plates. He seldom locked the doors, kept the keys behind the visor and put off getting the brakes fixed because he didn't want to spend the money.

He was in some ways the commonest of men. His home number was in the book; he answered the phone himself. He owned a business jet but routinely flew commercial coach class.

His favorite restaurant was McDonald's, where he invariably ordered french fries. He was a member of the exclusive Arid Club, but seldom ate there because he thought the prices were too high. Of far more interest to him was the club's card room. His game: gin rummy, no holds barred.

"Life was a game for him," his son Scott said. "One deal was followed by the next. You reshuffled the cards and went on to the next hand."

He liked cards, skiing, golf, duck hunting, McDonald's french fries, derby hats, Lincolns, horses and red licorice. He easily out-calculated opponents at the card table, effortlessly added large sums in his head — and could count on his fingers the number of books he had read. The bibles on his nightstand were Business Week, Fortune, Forbes, Time, U.S. News & World Report, National Geographic and Reader's Digest.

He had more money than some banks but drove old cars, hunted for golf balls, saved used nails, wore the same pair of glasses for more than 30 years and never failed to collect on a bet.

"He bet me 50 cents on the Yankees-Dodgers World Series when I was little," his daughter, Gay, said. "He took the Yankees. Fifty cents was a lot for me then. And he collected!"

Rightly known as a tough businessman, he was a shrewd entrepreneur with a genius for seeing an opportunity, taking a risk and turning a profit. He once foreclosed on a business loan to one of his own sons. Richard Simplot shrugged it off as part of doing business with his father, but some were rankled by the elder Simplot's freewheeling entrepreneurial streak.

"He was a bottom-line guy," rancher and former state legislator John Peavey said. "It didn't sit well with a lot of people when he moved a good part of his operation down to Washington and Oregon, where there's a longer growing season and lower electrical rates. That hasn't been a good thing for Idaho's potato industry."

In the 1970s, Simplot's support for building coal-fired power plants along the Snake River and for generating hydropower by putting the North Fork of the Payette River in an underground tube was anathema to environmentalists.

"That river is a destination objective for people from all over the world to test their whitewater skills," said Boisean Rob Lesser, a founder of the Idaho Whitewater Association. "When I heard about the plan to put it in a tunnel, I was literally sick."

Environmentalist Pat Ford, a former director of the Idaho Conservation League, squared off with the J.R. Simplot Co. on numerous occasions, seldom successfully.

"He and his company have not been environmental stewards for Idaho's lands and waters," Ford said. "They were consistent opponents of efforts to strengthen Idaho's air quality and land-use laws. And more often than not, they won."

Attempts to pigeonhole Simplot as a ruthless opportunist, however, fail to reflect the paradoxes of a man who could seem simple and one-dimensional but was neither. The wheeler-dealer who wanted to harness a whitewater river seldom failed to comment on the beauty of a forest, a flower garden or a desert sunset. He was a workaholic who spent relatively little time with his children — his two oldest boys were educated at a series of distant boarding schools — but compensated for it by doting on his grandchildren. When Richard Simplot, who died in 1993, was hospitalized for diabetic complications, the father who foreclosed on him was the first at his bedside. And late in life, the tough businessman was given to tearful reminiscences of the day he married his first wife and the time when, as a tow-headed boy from Declo, he saw Buffalo Bill.

His longtime friend H. Dean Summers saw Simplot's softer side during a helicopter trip with his old friend.

"When you're out with Jack, you always eat where he has an establishment, and we landed at one of his ranches where they were rounding up horses," he said. "We had our hunting clothes on, and the cowboys didn't know who we were. They brought in a horse with a huge cut on its front shoulder. It was 6 inches long and filled with pus.

"When the foreman said to take the horse out and shoot it, Jack jumped down from a plank of the corral and asked for a veterinary kit.

He cleaned out the wound with his bare hands and stitched it up with an old needle. When I asked him why, when he had 500 other horses, he said that horse had as much right to live as anybody."

He cited as his greatest accomplishment his refusal to sell the company he founded. It had its beginnings in 1928, when the flip of a silver dollar gave 19-year-old Jack Simplot his partner's half of an electric potato sorter. The machine speeded up work enough that Simplot's Declo neighbors eagerly sought its services. One sorter led to four, one potato shed to 33, and an empire was born.

If the coin had come down tails, the story probably wouldn't have ended much differently. A born gambler on the beginning of an incredible roll, Simplot already had provided ample evidence of the combination of horse sense and entrepreneurial vision that would make him Idaho's potato king.

"From the very beginning, he was a risk-taker," former Gov. John Evans said. "If he found something he believed in, no one could sway him from it. He saw opportunities, bet on himself and usually won."

Born on Jan. 4, 1909, to Charles and Dorothy Simplot on an Iowa homestead, he was one of six children. He was still in diapers when the family moved to Declo in Cassia County. His father built a log cabin and cleared land with a team of horses.

Except for 1919 to 1921, when his father experimented with farming in California and Oregon, Idaho was Simplot's home for life. His early years revolved around classes at the two-room Red Rock School and work on the family farm.

"You had to get up at 5 o'clock every morning and start milking those goddamned cows, and then you walked to school a mile or two, and then you run home to get more chores," he recalled. "That old man of mine was a hard driver."

It was a hard, make-do life. When young J.R. lost a fingertip in an accident and a doctor in Burley admonished his parents for not bringing it to be reattached, they told him the chickens had eaten it.

The legacy of hard work, however, remained for life. Even his donations could come with expectations attached. He contributed part of what was needed; others could come up with the rest.

"He worked hard and expected everyone else to work hard," his son Don said. "He about worked my brother and me to death clearing trails at McCall. I couldn't wait to get my own place and get out from under that."

At 14, the future billionaire got out from under his own father's authoritarian rule. When Charles Simplot refused to let him attend a basketball game, J.R. left home and moved to the Enyeart Hotel in Declo.

With money he made raising orphaned lambs, he purchased interest-bearing scrip at 50 cents on the dollar from teachers living at the hotel and used it as collateral to buy 600 hogs. He got them through the winter by shooting wild horses and boiling their meat with potato scraps to make feed. The summer brought a nationwide pork shortage, and he sold the hogs for a $7,800 profit — his stake in the potato business.

An innovator from the start, he leased land and bought certified seed instead of using the then-common practice of planting potato culls. The result was better potatoes and the beginning of Idaho's dominance in the industry.

In 1931, Simplot married Ruby Rosevear of Glenns Ferry. They met on a blind date; he proposed to her in his Model A Ford.

"She was beautiful," Adelia Simplot, Richard's widow, said. "She was quiet and introverted and wanted a simple life. She hated anything that was showy. He was very much in love with her."

Ruby Simplot's simple life wasn't to be. Nine years after marrying her, Simplot owned 30,000 acres of farm and ranch land and was shipping 10,000 boxcars of potatoes a year. Other Idahoans took their families to the mountains for vacation; Simplot took his to a feedlot. Grand View, where the company farms and feeds up to 150,000 head of cattle, was his Shangri-la. Family outings almost invariably had a business connection.

He celebrated his success by making extravagant purchases and hobnobbing with Averell Harriman, Lowell Thomas and other celebrities at Sun Valley.

"He was a dapper dresser, and he had the best cars, the best airplanes, the best of everything," Don Simplot said. "Later, he reverted. He found he got more strokes by being rich and having old stuff: 'Goddammit, who needs a new car? They cost too damned much money.'"

As a father, his primary roles were to provide discipline and financial support. The children went to the best schools. When Richard was diagnosed with juvenile-onset diabetes, his father saw to it that he had the best care in the region. But the head of the house was seldom at home. Empire-building came first.

Potatoes led to onions and a quantum leap in the Simplot fortune. With a contract scrawled on the back of an envelope, Simplot had an order for 500,000 pounds of dried onions and an immediate need for a plant to process them. He wanted to build it at Parma, but a man with a deed to the land sicced his dogs on Simplot, and he settled on Caldwell instead. The Caldwell plant, eventually equipped with the world's largest food dehydrator, was key to his operation, becoming the largest supplier of potatoes to the military during World War II. It supplied one of every three potato portions served to U.S. troops.

But it was the french fry that became the Simplot mainstay. In the early 1950s, company chemist Ray Dunlap developed the world's first palatable frozen fries. Sales began slowly in 1953, then skyrocketed.

The boss's enthusiasm for potatoes — in any form — was limitless.

"I met him when Dick took me to his parents' house after a date one night," said Adelia Simplot. "Ruby could see that Dick and I wanted to be together, but all J.R. wanted to do was make potatoes. The company had just come up with mashed potatoes in a packet, and he was all excited about them. He put butter on them, and we had to eat them."

By 1955, the year the company incorporated all of its operations under the name J.R. Simplot Co., annual french fry production exceeded 10 million pounds. A handshake with McDonald's founder Ray Kroc on Kroc's California ranch in 1967 made Simplot the supplier of nearly half the McDonald's fries sold worldwide. By then, he was Idaho's first billionaire.

The Simplot touch wasn't uniformly golden, however. Food-processing operations in Europe and mining investments in South America, the Caribbean and North Idaho either failed to show a profit or lost money. The successes in World War II were tempered by a $2.5 million tax bill and an order to dismantle partnerships that the Internal Revenue Service judged to be tax dodges.

A generation later, Simplot was charged with trying to manipulate Maine potato futures, barred from commodities trading for six years and fined $50,000. In 1977, he and his company paid $40,000 each for failing to report more than $1 million in corporate income and claiming false tax deductions.

Seemingly unfazed, he continued to extol the virtues of America and free enterprise. An American flag flies over every Simplot operation, and a flag said to have been the largest in Idaho rippled in the wind high above the 7,000-square-foot home he built in the hills overlooking Boise. When neighbors complained that its flapping kept them awake nights, he bought a taller flagpole.

In his sunset years, however, the man with the big flag was unable to vote. He confided that it was the most painful consequence of the felony tax conviction. And the pressures of empire-building took a toll on his personal life.

To rest after marathon work sessions during the company's formative years, he turned to sleeping medications and became dependent on them. Before kicking the habit, he was buying over-the-counter sleeping pills in pint bottles.

Work demands and time away from home created problems no amount of money or enthusiasm could fix. Ruby Simplot left him in 1960 after 29 years of marriage.

"I was too busy when I lost my first wife, and she fell in love with somebody else," he said in 1982. "That was one of the darkest times of my life."

"He suffered greatly," Adelia Simplot said. "His heart was broken. We all went through it with him."

The treatment was one for which he was uniquely qualified.

"He got through it by working," she continued. "He'd get on a horse and clear trails and work himself half to death. Work was his medicine."

His cure was Esther Becker.

Simplot met her during a business trip to New York in the mid '60s. She was a receptionist with the Henry Phipps Foundation. They saw a show together; the following year, he invited her to a play. He slept through it, but she continued to see him anyway. In 1968, after visiting him in Idaho, she moved to Denver. They were married Jan. 22, 1972, in McCall.

Esther Becker Simplot graduated from MacMurray College in Jacksonville, Ill. She majored in voice and music education, and she had sung in operas in New York City. She broadened Simplot's appreciation of the arts, but his penchant for sleeping through a ballet or opera was lifelong.

When he retired in 1994 as company chairman, he gave the family leadership to a four-person executive committee consisting of his daughter, surviving sons and a grandson. The senior Simplot stayed on as chairman emeritus. He remained a familiar figure in the executive offices, habitually napping in a room specially reserved for the purpose, but ever alert to new possibilities. At 87, having ceded much of the company's control, he unsuccessfully pitched the purchase of a 3 million-acre ranch in Australia.

"It reminded him of Grand View," his grandson, John Otter, Butch's son, said. "He said from there we could grow anything and feed that whole part of the world. 'Hell, he said, 'we could grow guacamole here!'"

Too busy to dote on his own children when they were young, he bought his grandchildren Welsh ponies, taught them to play cards and ride horses, took them skiing and golfing, and gave them their own development company.

"He was making up for the time he missed with us," Don Simplot said. "There's no doubt about that."

In his 90s, he seldom missed a Micron board meeting and was often seen about town on his scooter, at events from Boise State University football games (he routinely bet $10 on the Broncos) to Art in the Park. In 70 years, he never missed a Caldwell Night Rodeo.

A garrulous extrovert who addressed women as "Honey" and middle-aged men as "Boy" or "Sonny," he seldom appeared to have a care in the world or anything negative to say about anyone or anything.

"I never saw him bad-mouth anyone, never saw him tell a dirty joke, and I never saw him get anything by saying he was Mr. Simplot and throwing his weight around," Summers said.

Employees generations younger than Simplot joked that he would outlive them all. He was rarely if ever sick. He had an artificial knee and hip, and he meant it when he vowed that as long as he had money and the doctors had spare parts, he'd be their best customer. He gave up skiing at 89 and was miffed when his doctors wouldn't let him attend a wedding in McCall a few days after coronary bypass surgery at 90.

He bought his first Wave Runner at 94.

"He rode it around Payette Lake and then had it moved to Grand View to ride on the Snake River after the lake had frozen," John Otter said. "He wanted to take his shotgun along so he could drive with one hand and shoot geese with the other."

That was the winter he turned 95.

He spent his 98th birthday in a Phoenix hospital after suffering a serious head injury in a fall at the Fiesta Bowl, but surprised nearly everyone by recovering from the resulting surgery, successfully completing his rehabilitation and returning home. He attributed his extraordinary health and longevity in part to abstinence from tobacco and alcohol. Taught a "lesson in booze" early in life by a hard-drinking business associate, he was reluctant to hire anyone who drank or smoked, gave

$200 to any employee who quit smoking and paid a former minister to travel the state in a bus, displaying black lungs while lecturing to high school students on the evils of tobacco.

He couldn't type or operate a computer, but he carried a Micron computer chip in his pocket. A hard-nosed pragmatist, he had little use for religion and called education "the only charity that I really support. I guess I'm a facts man."

He contributed millions of dollars to education and supported his children's and grandchildren's educational preferences, but he didn't insist that they go to college. Mostly, he just wanted them to work hard.

"I learned the value of hard work from my father and grandfather," John Otter said. "One summer, I got a job as a construction worker at Micron without his help. Toward the end of the summer, one of the construction workers, when he found out who I was, said, 'You gotta thank your parents and your granddad. You were born with a silver spoon, and you used it to dig a ditch.'"

If Simplot had gotten a degree instead of dropping out of grade school, it would have been in business. A businessman, he often said, can do anything.

Asked how he wanted to be remembered, his response was typical Simplot: "Oh, hell, I don't care what they say. But I think I've made enough marks around here that somebody will say, 'Well, that guy was pretty smart. He hung on.'"

He did, for nearly a century — as the state's leading industrialist and arguably its most colorful character.

"He did more for Idaho than anybody, and he did it the old-fashioned way," Summers said. "There probably aren't 50 people in America who have built companies and wealth the way he did, and no one's done it in the last 25 years. He owned it all. There were no shareholders, because he didn't need them.

"I saw him run 150 yards down a muddy hill on a duck-hunting trip when he was 91 and had just had bypass surgery. He was the toughest S.O.B. God ever let live."

'He should be a superstar'
(July 6, 2007)

Pinto Bennett in his "retirement home," a sheep wagon in a lonely stretch of Owyhee County. (Darin Oswald / Idaho Statesman)

It's quitting time at Shorty's Saloon and Pinto Bennett has the blues. He orders bourbon as a reward for sticking with water during his sets and resumes a conversation begun during his break.

"All my life people have been telling me I'm ahead of my time," he says. "It'd be nice if the times would be right for once."

His voice is subdued, almost as if in atonement for his years of honky tonk living. His blue eyes have lost some of their fire, his red beard has gone white and his once bullish physique has dropped 60 pounds. It's hard to believe this gentle poet could once have been the barrel-chested hell-raiser who partied like a fleet sailor and in a haze of LSD carved a name in ballpoint pen on the front of a prized vintage guitar.

The reformed Pinto Bennett talks freely about the old one.

"I've had a stroke and four heart attacks. When I was in the hospital after the first one, I saw a preacher on the television and decided I didn't want to live like I had been all my life. I haven't done drugs since. I'm an alcoholic, but I'm getting better. I thank God I became a Christian. If I hadn't, I'd be dead now."

As Fridays go, it's a slow night at Shorty's. Bennett has seen enough slow nights that he's written a song about them, one of more than 200 he's registered. He knows many of the customers personally. A smile that could light a dark stage lights his tired face as he bids them what has become his standard farewell.

"God bless you. Adios."

The softness of his speaking voice is in startling contrast to the power of his singing. He rarely sings a song he hasn't written, doesn't take requests for songs by other songwriters unless they're his personal favorites and dresses to please himself. His unvarying stage attire: blue jeans, white shirt and beige cowboy hat, string tie and gray cardigan sweater. His five-year-old Bolin acoustic guitar is worn through its finish from picking and amplified with an ancient pickup that's survived spilled drinks, onstage brawls and shows from Shorty's to Nashville.

Though he was never a Tim McGraw or a Kenny Chesney, listeners who recognize an original voice amid the conformity of pop country music know exactly who he is.

Jazz singer Curtis Stigers calls Bennett "the real deal and an Idaho treasure."

Folk singer-songwriter Rosalie Sorrels, sometimes called a treasure herself, says simply that "he should be a superstar."

Opinions vary on why he isn't. Some blame the fickleness of the business, some his past excesses, some his refusal to compromise his music. No one disputes his talent.

Nashville guitarist Sergio Webb, who has performed with Bennett off and on for 26 years, calls him "one of a handful of people you use as the standard. Is this as good as a Pinto song? Is this a good enough song to show Pinto? He's that kind of an influence. Even though he never made it here, he left a huge mark on Nashville."

His greatest success was in Europe, where sudden fame was the reverse of his experience in the U.S. Pinto Bennett and the Famous Motel Cowboys played two consecutive years at London's Wembley Country Music Festival, which has hosted Willie Nelson, Crystal Gayle, Hank Williams and other country legends. He drew crowds of 15,000, partied with the Everly Brothers, introduced Bonnie Raitt to chewing tobacco.

Now 59, he's happy to be a third of Trio Pinto with Boiseans Brett Dewey and Bill Parsons. His career has come full circle, from Idaho honky tonks to Albert Hall and back.

In 1989, riding high from playing at packed concerts in five European countries, he and his band returned to the U.S. and were fired for not playing any Alabama songs on their first job, at a bar in Rock Springs, Wyo. He laughs when he tells the story, but only briefly. A microcosm of his life, it cuts close to the bone.

In a book of song lyrics and reminiscences, Bennett wrote that he was "living proof that in Nashville it ain't who you know that counts. I know everyone and couldn't get nothin' goin'. ... I found out that I was an old sheep-camp pickup in a lot full of BMWs."

The sheep-camp metaphors come honestly. Born Frederick Robert Bennett in Iowa in 1947, he all but grew up in a sheep camp in Elmore County. His parents moved to Mountain Home when he was a year old to be closer to his father's family. They named him after his sheep-rancher grandfather for whom the onetime community of Bennett, near the Little Camas Reservoir, was named.

"I was the ugliest little kid you ever saw; I had freckles all over me. My brother and I listened to a guy named Pinto Colvig (the voice of Disney's Goofy) on the record player, and that's how I picked the name. Grampa said it was better than being called Spot."

Little Pinto helped with the camp chores and learned from the herders to speak some Basque and Spanish. Spanish occasionally flavors his lyrics.

I said I'd eat my hat if you left me like that.
Juevos rancheros sombrero.

When he was old enough to handle a horse, he worked for his grandfather as a shepherd. One night he rode like a boy possessed to find that a train had killed some of the sheep. The incident inspired a song about the futile optimism of ranching life.

It was drizzling rain, I remember
That night the train hit the sheep.
Draggin' 'em off of old Nedberry Grade,
Tears and blood on my sweater,
Next year better.

His father, an amateur musician and would-be journalist with a weakness for cowboy bars, bought him his first pawn-shop guitar and introduced him to the honky-tonk lifestyle. Bennett remembers sleeping under shuffleboard machines and getting drunk with ranchers while they made bets on who would have the fattest sheep. He was then 9 years old.

His life changed the first time he heard Elvis singing "That's All Right" on a friend's record player

"I melted. My first memory of being alive is of the sheep camp. My first memory of being me is Elvis."

His first paying gig, "before whiskers," was in the early '60s with a band at a drive-in-restaurant in Mountain Home. He made $12.50. Soon he was sporting a ducktail and learning every song he could by his early heroes — Elvis, Hank Williams, Buck Owens, Conway Twitty and the Everly Brothers. The first song he wrote, "She's My Girl," was a regional hit in the early '60s by a Boise rock band called the Motifs.

His musical apprenticeship was progressing nicely when, at 17, he got into a scrape he won't discuss except to say he was "just havin' too much fun." A Mountain Home judge agreed and introduced him to the local Navy recruiter.

Bennett took to the Navy lifestyle the way a sailor takes to waterfront bars. He has four anchor tattoos and a peacock that stretches from his belt buckle to his heart, played in a band with a clever but unprintable nautical name, partied in ports from Long Beach to Naples. He loved serving aboard the cruiser Topeka, but a transfer to a destroyer devastated him. He hated life on the destroyer so much that he rejected a rare offer to apply at the Naval Academy in favor of playing music.

"I was gonna' be the next Elvis," he said.

After his discharge as a bosun's mate — he ruefully admits to making third-class twice — he enrolled at Idaho State University. It took him three days to decide it was a waste of time, drop out and spend the rest of his G.I. Bill money on rent for a band house. The following year, 1971, he moved to Boise and co-founded a band named for a friend, Bud Tarwater. Its bumper stickers described it perfectly: "Tarwater — Hard Country Music."

Tarwater played music from outlaw country to hard-core rock and roll. The group survived multiple incarnations and most of the '70s.

Bennett and his wife of 32 years spent the late '70s and early '80s living in a sheep wagon near his boyhood haunts at Bennett.

"Those are my fondest memories of him," Barbara Bennett said. "The other guys in the band would bring home friends. He'd bring home winos and ask if we had anything for them to eat."

He built a bar out of native rock beside the sheep wagon, played there with the Pinto Bennett Band and, in her words, "had his seven-year itch 15 years late."

154

The "itch" was a rodeo queen. He and Barbara were divorced, but later remarried. The bar was sold.

"I blew it," he said. "I was my own best customer."

The light at the bottom of the bottle proved to be the Famous Motel Cowboys, formed in 1987. First-rate musicians with enough original Bennett songs to fill a guitar case, they didn't even know it when they had a hit that summer in England.

"One night a friend called from England and said, 'hey, your record's a big deal here.' Sergio (Webb) and I decided to go over and check it out."

Bennett and Webb arrived in London that October, nearly broke. A friend who was working as the Everly Brothers' road manager came to their rescue with deluxe accommodations in Kensington Gardens. From barely being able to afford a room, the motel cowboys went to hanging out with the Everly Brothers at Albert Hall and watching Bennett's "Valuable Time," co-written with cowboy poet Baxter Black, become a hit.

Work was all I thought about when we were man and wife.
I was always just one step behind the Joneses' life.
... Then one empty midnight, I came in to find you gone.
You took the kids, and you took the car and you took my last dime.
And left me with nothing but my valuable time.

"Sergio and I would entertain the Everlys after their show, which was incredible because they'd been my heroes forever. We opened for Willie and Waylon and Crystal Gayle."

He paused, laughed ...

"I put a big lip lock on her, and she kissed me back! We toured in England, Ireland, Scotland, Germany and France that summer. We were the Eagles, man! They'd have Pinto Bennett hours on the radio stations. After that, I lived in London off and on for the next few years."

If England was the "on," Nashville was the "off." Hoping to make it as a songwriter, Bennett moved there in the early '90s and set up shop — sheep-camp style.

"He was living in a horse trailer with a bed and a chair in it," Barbara Bennett said. "But he was drinking less and wasn't pretending to be a redneck anymore. He'd turned his life around. If he hadn't, I never would have married him again."

He spent a total of five years in Nashville, most of them in a rented house just off of Music Row. He and the band performed and recorded whenever they could. The Idahoans earned Nashville's respect, but not its acceptance.

"It takes a long time," Webb said by phone from his Nashville home. "You need somebody to run interference, you need a manager, you almost need divine intervention."

Though he was never a Nashville star, Bennett's personal magnetism made him a Nashville character. He is gregarious, witty, disarmingly likeable. Everyone who knows him has a favorite Pinto story. He'll talk about anything from his alcoholism to his sex life with directness that initially stuns people and within seconds has them laughing. Like another Idaho character, J.R. Simplot, he's all but incapable of not using creative profanity, of which he is seemingly unaware. Even the priggish tend to overlook it because it's who he is.

"He has a goodness and sincerity about him," Sorrels said. "... Everyone I know in Nashville who knows him loves him."

His Nashville friends covered the spectrum from his band members and their families to a mentally disabled man at the hotel that gave him a job as a night manager — he was big, strong and had a gun — to some of the city's musical legends. When Chet Atkins played at Boise's Morrison Center in 1995, he wished the crowd well from his Idaho friend Pinto Bennett in Nashville. Bennett's mother, who was in the audience, wept.

His drinking buddies included Don Everly, Townes Van Zandt and Lyle Lovett. He laughs about the time a Nashville newcomer told him he was going to be the next George Strait.

"Kid, this is Nashville," Bennett told him. "Go back home to Oklahoma and get a producer and a whole bunch of money. He did, and the rest is history."

The kid was Garth Brooks.

The child in Bennett's life at the time was the youngest of his three daughters, Danielle, now 21. Danielle grew up around some of country's biggest stars, but says it "wasn't a big thing because that was just my life, and Dad was just my dad. He took me to school every day. He never once let me take the bus. He took me on all my field trips, taught me to ride a bike, taught me how to drive. Even with all the gigs, he always had time for me."

While her husband pursued his musical dream, Barbara Bennett worked as a waitress at a motel and a restaurant. When he wasn't writing or performing, Pinto helped pay the bills by working as a tree trimmer, a plumber's assistant and doing odd jobs.

But the dream remained out of reach.

"All the songwriters came to see me. If Bob Dylan was in town, he'd have been there. I *am* Pinto Bennett. They knew I was somebody; I commanded some respect. But if you don't get a record deal …

"They want you to be cute, lose weight, quit drinkin'. … I wanted to do it my way."

Barbara Bennett remembers it a bit differently:

"They want short, sweet stories in Nashville. He wanted to say it all and said it well, but that wasn't what they wanted to hear. His lyrics almost tell too much."

He is a man haunted by words.

Boise singer Belinda Bowler, who dated one of the Famous Motel Cowboys while she was touring England in the '80s, remembers their front man "constantly scribbling lyrics on crumpled-up pieces of paper. He'd scribble, doze off, wake up and scribble some more. I remember thinking it was like constantly grinding gears. He's always doing his craft. He just works and works and works. That's part of what makes him such a masterful songwriter."

The lights in his West Boise mobile home routinely are on most of the night.

"I can't sleep. That's part of why I drink so much; I can't shut my brain off. I'm always thinking about songs. I'll stay up all night working on lyrics."

For a songwriter mainly known for country music, he cites unexpectedly diverse influences — Elvis, Jimi Hendrix, the Beatles, The Band, Chuck Berry, Carl Perkins ... When he gets an idea for a lyric, he scrawls it on an index card and puts it in a folder. When the folder is fat enough, he peruses the cards and decides which words work together.

"I don't even get the guitar out. I have it figured out in my brain, even the style and melody, before I ever play it. To me, it's always been about the words. That's why I think so many songs today are so stupid. They might have a good hook, but they just drive it into the dirt."

The front room where he works is decorated with paintings and photographs — ships, sheepwagons, cowboys, Nashville, London. Cowboy hats and a VFW cap dangle from a rack beside the door. Bennett regularly plays at the Garden City VFW post, where he's a member. An American flag and a "God Bless America" sticker overlook the kitchen table, where he spent three hours answering questions during an interview in April. Midway through, he unscrewed the lid from a half-gallon jug of paisano wine and began taking slugs, cowboy-style, tilting the bottle over his shoulder.

"I've given up everything but this since I became a Christian," he said. "I still drink, but I'm gettin' better. I'm cognizant of what I'm doing now. ... There's no doubt that drinking hurt my career. A lot of people didn't pay attention to my soul or what I had to offer. They just thought I was a drunk."

My mind's lost all feeling, the wine keeps it reeling,
Helping my heart take the fall.
I'm mad as a hatter, and it's wine over matter,
But it's better than nothing at all.

The onetime drug user, binge drinker and author of a ribald book and semi-autobiographical song titled "Honky Tonk Asshole" is now a regular at the Collister Community Church.

Pastor Corbett Lynn — the preacher he saw on television after his first heart attack — says a simple message changed the motel cowboy's hard-country lifestyle.

"I told him we're sinners and we can't change that, but salvation is a free gift when we accept Christ," Lynn said. "I think he's done that."

Bennett sings at church, plays for free enough that he jokes his name should be Pinto Benefit, and seldom goes a week without doing volunteer work. He doesn't talk about it — he considers it bragging — but the fans at one of his 44 Club charity jam sessions were happy to share stories: Bennett and his family hosting holiday dinners and collecting coats for school children and the Boise Rescue Mission, Bennett pushing wheelchair-bound patients around the VA hospital, Bennett playing Santa at military installations and nursing homes. With his white beard, rosy cheeks and gentle blue eyes, he could almost do it without the costume.

Mike Gough, a 23-year-old Boise filmmaker, says his mother was needlessly horrified when a younger, more notorious Bennett moved into the trailer next door to theirs.

"I was in third grade, and Mom had heard lots of stories about the most famous motel cowboy of them all. She told me to stay away from him. I never met my real dad, though, and after a while he became like a father to me. He told me about mistakes he made that helped me steer clear of bad influences. And whenever I had a band performance or a play at school, he was always there. At this point, I'd have to say that he is my father."

Gough flew to Nashville in March to film the recording of a Tarwater reunion CD. He's raising money in hopes of making a full-length movie on Bennett's career, and some of Bennett's songs are enjoying a Texas revival with new renditions by Austin-based Reckless Kelly and Mickey and the Motorcars.

"He's one of the best songwriters out there," Reckless Kelly's Cody Braun said. "His songs are always on the cutting edge of what you can get away with, which is what kept him off of country radio. He's so honest and straightforward. I think he could make it in Austin."

Bennett is flattered, as he is by fans who urge him to give the big time another shot. But, like his worn guitar, he's old beyond his years. He takes a handful of prescription medications daily. His stroke left him almost deaf in one ear and legally blind in one eye. He lost his driver's license because of it and has become a familiar figure walking the streets of West Boise and Garden City. He walks up to 10 miles a day, often stopping to visit with homeless people.

He doesn't dwell on not making it big in the U.S. and says with a straight face that his biggest regret was not being a guest on the Muppet Show. Being a superstar has never been as important to him as writing songs thoughtful listeners appreciate.

"It's nice at my age that people think I might still have a chance," he said. "The kids are startin' to discover my songs, and that's nice. I'd go on Austin City Limits if they asked me, but they won't and I don't care. I'm tired. I've started over enough. ... I'll probably be a millionaire after I'm dead, and that's OK, too. I've made peace with it."

For the past year, he's been working part-time as a welder's helper at what he aptly calls the boneyard, a weedy back lot strewn with moribund vehicles in Garden City.

One is an ancient Farm-All tractor, like the one his grandfather used at the sheep camp. Another is a trailer. He calls them his retirement package. He plans to build a sheepwagon on the trailer and pull it with the tractor around the hills and prairies of Bennett, where he learned to herd sheep and play the guitar and wants to return in his old age.

"That's my dream," he said. "You don't need a driver's license for a tractor. I'll take it to all the old places and hang out in it. It'll be like being at the sheep camp again, only better. I won't have any sheep."

IDAHO PLACES

The Rainbow Bridge crosses the North Fork of the Payette River and attracts photographers and artists with its beauty. (Pete Zimowsky / Idaho Statesman)

A former Statesman editor once joked that there was "no corner of the state Woodward hasn't trod." It was almost true. From Boise to hamlets with names like Bone and Small and Good Grief to the eerie beauty of Silver City in the dead of winter, I was lucky enough to visit virtually every corner of Idaho and get paid for it. The stories that follow are among the results.
— Tim Woodward

General Store Extraordinaire
(July 26, 1979)

PICABO – The mottled hills and green fields of Picabo (pronounced peek-a-boo) seem an unlikely place for commercial enterprise. The nearest town of any size is Carey (population 300), six miles to the east. The more populous towns of Hailey and Ketchum are half an hour away on a narrow country road.

Picabo itself has a population of about 50. A man with a good arm could throw a rock from the center of town to the Holsteins that graze in the nearby pastures.

There is a commercial enterprise in Picabo, though, and you see it long before you get to town. It's an uncertain color, somewhere between red and lavender, and on a clear day it's visible for miles in each direction. The two words painted in white on the west side can be read from a distance of half a mile, and they don't lie. The place is a bona fide "General Store," the only one of its kind in the state.

I've seen my share of stores, from Mom and Pop operations to Harrod's, but I've never seen anything quite like the General Store at Picabo.

If it's legal, you can get it there.

On the left, as you walk in the front door, is the outdoorsmen's department.

At this time of year there is only a token concession to hunters – mostly in the form of ammunition – but the famous Silver Creek is close by and the fishing section is formidable. You can get anything from a gray hackle to a spinning reel or a pair of chest waders. If you need a hat, sunglasses or tanning lotion, they have those, too.

Walk half a dozen steps and you're in the grocery section. The General Store is about half the size of a typical supermarket, but I'd be surprised if a supermarket sells something it doesn't. It has dry goods, canned foods, produce, pet foods, kitchen utensils, greeting cards, drugs, detergent, beer, wine, paper products, pastries, you name it. You can buy anything from a fresh pineapple to a can of minced clams to a plastic fly swatter.

The grocery section is more or less the middle of the store. The front of the store resembles an upper level in a department store. It has small appliances – blenders, electric can openers, toaster ovens, deep fryers, electric ice cream makers and the like – and an assortment of other products that vary widely in types and sizes.

It is possible, in this part of the store, to purchase anything from a pair of socks to a carpet shampooer. You can pick up towels for the bathroom, sheets for the bedroom, pottery and glassware for the kitchen, a clock for the living room and knickknacks for the dining room. When you're finished, you can buy a camera to take a picture of it all.

The rear of the store is reserved for harder stuff. You can get a number 14 bucket there. You can get an edger for your sidewalk or a set of shoes for your horse. Plumbers and electricians will find enough wire, pipe and gadgets to last several lifetimes.

Carpenters can buy anything from hammers and nails to jigsaws and electric sanders. Gardeners will find whatever they need, from pruning shears right on up to lawnmowers. You can pick up a new set of tires for your car; you can purchase a replacement for your water heater.

The General Store at Picabo is the only place I know where you can get African violet food, alfalfa seed, panty hose, a chain saw, water chestnuts, a horse bridle, paperback books, a hundred pounds of wheat, a bottle of perfume, a dozen eggs and a load of lumber in one stop.

While you wait for the lumber to be loaded, you can sit down in one of the two booths at the front of the store and be served a hot sandwich and a soft drink. On your way out, you can mail a letter (the southwest corner of the General Store is a post office), and, in parting, fill your car's tank at one of the pumps out front. A person could spend a lifetime within driving distance of the General Store and, barring medical emergencies, never have to go anywhere else.

The manager and part owner of the place is Gordon Eccles, a fast-talking, no-nonsense man with a cluttered desk and a phone that doesn't stop ringing.

Eccles, who answered my questions between long distance calls and inquiries from employees, said Picabo began in the 1880s as a railroad stop and farm center. The name, he said, comes from an Indian word meaning shining waters, most likely a reference to Silver Creek. The store was built in 1952. It serves tourists but relies primarily on the country farm trade from Bellevue east.

"There are a lot of stores in out-of-the-way places in this state, but none as diversified as this," he said. "This is a true general store. We deliver fuel, feed and seed all over the county, and we have regular customers who come from 20 miles or more."

I don't know which was more unexpected – to find this clearing house for just-about-everything out in the middle of nowhere or to meet a man like Eccles there. Maybe it was just an unusually busy day, but he seemed as if he would have been more at home on Wall Street.

I didn't want to take too much of his time, but on the way out the door I thought of one last question and quickly asked if there was anything his store didn't sell.

He put his calls on hold, thought for about 10 seconds, and replied affirmatively.

"Yes, come to think of it there is. We don't sell cars."

Last Holdout
(April 26, 1979)

MONTOUR – As recently as 1975, Montour boasted a population of close to 100. Today it is moribund. Its school, community club, church and onetime homes are empty, their windows nailed shut with plywood that still hasn't weathered. You can stand in the middle of town and hear nothing but songbirds and the wind in the trees.

The town belongs to nature – grass, weeds and insects are taking over – and to the U.S. government, which has spared little effort in affixing its name, and its prosecutorial powers, to anything capable of holding up a no-trespassing sign.

Montour is a low spot in a valley surrounded by bare hills and intersected by the Payette River. The river is partly responsible for the town's demise. Since 1924, when Black Canyon Dam was constructed, Montour's people have fought the annual floodwaters that inundate the valley and, increasingly, the town. Silt continues to build up behind the dam, gradually filling the reservoir and extending the range of its backwaters. Each year the flood threat grows.

In 1975, after litigation and considerable controversy, the U.S. Bureau of Reclamation decided the cheapest way to further the common good was to buy the town, relocate its people, and let nature take its course.

A white frame house stands out among the ghosts. The grass is cut, tulips bloom in the front yard, tools line the fence around the recently planted vegetable garden. Outdoor Christmas lights cling to the siding above the front door. Inside, Esther Palmer, age 80, tends to her daily affairs. She is the last holdout.

Only two property owners have refused to sell. Alva McConnel still owns his 320 acres, but he lives down the valley, out of the town proper. Mrs. Palmer and her daughter, Frances, are all that is left of what was once Montour, Idaho (population: 2).

Frances's eyes narrow when visitors ask to see her mother.

"Are you from the bureau? If you're not from the bureau, you can come in."

The head of the house is seated in a kitchen chair with an orange tom cat on her lap. Esther Palmer says you're "only as old as you feel." From appearances, she feels about 25. Her brown eyes are piercing, her hair is mostly black, her hearing is as good as a teen-ager's.

"I never asked the government to buy me out," she said. "All I want is for them to let me alone."

Let alone, she and Frances are self-sufficient. They grow virtually all the common vegetables, tend a small flock of sheep, raise chickens and gather fruit from the trees that dot their 11 acres. Last year they put up 1,200 bales of hay.

"If you give me good land and good water, I'll make a living," Mrs. Palmer said. "I don't ask for any handouts. We get along very nicely here. If they move me into town, they'll have to put me on welfare."

All the neighbors have moved to town – mostly Emmett, 15 miles southwest – or to higher ground, in the valley but distant enough not to be neighbors anymore. Mrs. Palmer doesn't mind the seclusion – she happily reports that the geese and pheasants moved in when the people and dogs moved out – but the proliferation of weeds, peeling paint and boarded windows angers and saddens her. Anger because the Youth Conservation Corps, charged with keeping up appearances, has done little to stop the deterioration. Sad because she hates to see what is happening to her home of nearly six decades.

She came in 1913, in a horse and buggy from Kansas, and settled with her parents in a home down the valley. Her parents, ironically, moved to Emmett after selling their valley home to the government, which proceeded to flood it by building Black Canyon Dam.

In 1921, she moved to Montour and was married the same year to Deane Palmer, a railroad man. They spent their married lives there, raised two daughters and a son and never had any desire to leave. When Deane died in 1971, she saw no reason to move. She has been there since she was a bride – 58 years in the same house.

It isn't as lonely as you'd think. In addition to the chores, she and Frances read, watch television and occasionally go to Emmett, Caldwell or Boise for entertainment. Former neighbors drop by from time to time, and hardly a week goes by without passers-by coming to the door to ask why all the buildings are boarded up.

The 11 acres are shared with the sheep and chickens, a dog, Zip, and an uncertain number of cats. The only animal allowed in the house is the orange tom, who goes by the name of Tim.

"At one time we had 13 cats," she said. "A lot of people left them when they moved out. We have to get rid of them – it costs so much to feed them – but what do you do when a starved cat comes along?"

Here the kitchen conversation was interrupted by a telephone call.

"Hello … No, it won't do you any good to talk to me. They're runnin' us all out of this valley, and I'll be next … Goodbye."

It was a siding salesman.

The government's salesmen have offered $63,000 for the property. Mrs. Palmer doesn't want to sell, but if she did, it wouldn't be for $63,000. With inflation increasing the already-high cost of real estate (high ground is selling for up to $10,000 an acre), she doesn't consider the government's offer equitable.

"The Bureau of Reclamation promised to relocate us as good or better," she said with a trace of bitterness. "Where could I get a house and 11 acres for $63,000?"

At first, the town united against the government. Eventually, Mrs. Palmer said, the bureau indicated that the property could be taken by condemnation and that the offered price might be the best the townspeople could do.

"People got scared." One by one, they left.

The government doesn't come around much anymore. An agent dropped by last fall, but Mrs. Palmer "told him off good," and he hasn't been back since.

His name was Phillip Goodsale.

"I don't think he liked it very good, what I said to him … but there's no place in this world for a meek person. The meek aren't gonna inherit the earth. The meek are gonna be crushed."

Goodsale says the bureau has always tried to be open with Mrs. Palmer, and that he doesn't recall her being "anything but lady-like."

She says she belongs to a church and tries to live a good life. She isn't afraid of living in a ghost town, nor is she particularly afraid of floods. Her property, she argues, is just high enough that the odds are against serious damage. The only thing she fears is condemnation.

"I love this town," she said. Here there was a slight pause. Her 80-year-old eyes looked wistfully out the kitchen window at the tangle of neglect that ends at her property line. A pheasant rose from a nearby field. "I just wish I knew that I could spend the rest of my life here."

The bird, vivid in the afternoon sun, flew across the fields, past the empty buildings and no-trespassing signs, and came to rest in the sagebrush, on higher ground.

Small, Idaho
(Aug. 6, 1989)

The Smalls from Small: Kevin Small, left, his sister-in-law, Sheila Small, and her 10-year-old daughter, Molly. (Kim Hughes / Idaho Statesman)

SMALL, Idaho – It's hard to say for certain which is the smallest town in Idaho, but it would be hard to beat Small. At one time, it was listed in Ripley's Believe it or Not as the smallest town in America.

The population then was 1 – the postmaster.

Last year, Small had a population explosion. An entire family moved into a house on a hill above town. No one lives in the town proper, which consists of an abandoned store and post office.

Travelers don't take the gravel road to Small by accident. I went there because (to borrow from George Leigh Mallory) it was there – a tiny, intriguing dot on the map.

Besides, it was only a small distance out of my way.

"If you want to know about Small," the woman in the house on the hill said, "go up the road to the second ranch on the left. The people there know all about it."

"Thanks. What's their name?"

"Small."

Lee Small has lived up the road from Small all his life. He and his wife, Mary, have a cattle and horse ranch. Their sons Kevin and Butch and their adopted son Marty Forester are cowboys.

Not just ordinary cowboys – rodeo cowboys. You don't expect to meet big names in a place like Small, but the Smalls' sons are famous. All have placed among the top 15 rodeo cowboys in the nation. Butch has been in the top 15 for seven consecutive years.

Lee invited me into their living room – its walls are literally covered with rodeo photos – and told me, among other things, how Small got its name.

"My granddad, Dennis Small, came here on his way west in 1881," he said. "He ran horses, too. He went on to Oregon but then came back, had 10 children and got the town named after him. There have been Smalls here for over 100 years."

"Do you like it here?" I asked him.

"Oh, I know there are better places to live. I don't like the winters, but I'm 69 and don't know anything else. And the kids turned out good.

They all went to college and haven't ever been in trouble. There's no crime here; we never lock our doors. Yeah, I guess I like it, all right."

We sat and talked for a spell; then the boys took me out back for a look at their bunkhouse.

The bunkhouse is like something out of a Roy Rogers movie – rifles hanging from log walls, boots and spurs lining the bunks, cowboy paraphernalia everywhere. You almost expect to see Gabby Hayes gumming a sourdough biscuit.

So where do the hands go when they need something from the 20th century?

"If it's small, we go to Dubois," Lee Small said. "If it's big, we go to the Falls (Idaho Falls)."

He laughed and added that there wasn't much point in going to Small.

"These ranches never did pay much, but in the old days people stayed and tried to make it. At its peak, there might have been 30 people who got their mail at Small. Now, you'll have one guy who owns three or four places and lives in the Falls or even Utah.

"We're the only original family left, and except for granddad the Smalls never were very productive. There aren't even many Smalls at Small anymore."

The Strangest House in Idaho
(June 27, 1990)

WALLACE – In a state as big as Idaho, it's just about impossible to travel to a Centennial event every day.

After finishing up with Worley Days on Sunday, for example, I could have gone to an Idaho Celebration on Monday and a Centennial tour on Tuesday.

But it would have meant driving from the Coeur d'Alene area to Franklin (in southeast Idaho) and back to Lewiston, a distance measured in light years.

The operative phrase when it was impractical to be at a Centennial event was "road color," journalese for interesting places, colorful characters, etc., along the route.

And few places in Idaho are more colorful than the Wallace home of Gary McKinnon.

McKinnon's cartoon world, clinging by its fingernails to a steep hillside overlooking this old mining town, may well be the strangest house in Idaho.

To get there, take the winding road that heads north out of town. Round a bend, pass a played-out mine and there it is: a cartoon house surrounded by cartoon characters, looking as unreal against the wooded slope as something from another planet.

The characters, three to four feet tall, are painted on pieces of plywood that follow a steep, wooden stairway to the house.

McKinnon has done them all – Mickey Mouse, Donald Duck, Goofy, Pluto, Snow White and the Seven Dwarfs, Cinderella, Alice in Wonderland, Pinocchio, Daffy Duck, Woody Woodpecker, Bugs Bunny, Elmer Fudd, the Wizard of Oz, ET … you get the idea.

The house itself is slightly less colorful – just your standard old house clinging to a cliff, with an eight-foot gyroscope on the roof and a flying saucer on the front deck.

The flying saucer would look more at home at a carnival. At least 15 feet across, it has a silver cockpit with circular windows and spokes extending outward to red and green lights that look like traffic signals.

The flying saucer spins, of course, as does the blue and white gyroscope on the roof.

People in town warned me that McKinnon, 57, was a recluse. On the other hand, what serious journalist could resist asking for an interview.

I climbed the creaking stairs and banged on the door. It opened a crack; a pair of gentle, darting eyes peered out from the darkness.

"Yes?"

I explained my business.

"Oh. What do you want to know?"

"Well, let's see. How long have you been working on all this?"

"Seventeen years."

"Where did you learn to paint?"

"I taught myself."

The door never opened more than a few inches. Every few seconds, the eyes looked back inside, as if looking for a place to hide.

"What do you do for a living?" I asked.

"Nothing right now. But I'm a roper."

"Roper?"

"Yes. I can rope things behind me without looking. Once I roped a post 24 feet behind me 55 times without missing."

"Is there much call for that?"

"No. That's why I'm not doing it."

"Where did you learn backwards roping?"

"It's supernatural."

This more or less concluded our interview.

I thanked McKinnon and was turning to leave when I thought of one last question.

"Why do you make all these things?"

"Because it pleases people," he said.

You can't argue with that.

Editor's note: This was written when Idaho was celebrating its Centennial and Tim took a tour of celebrations around the state.

The Museum of Just-About-Everything
(July 12, 1998)

OWYHEE COUNTY — Jack Lawson's junk collection is an Owyhee County wonder. But he never dreamed it would become a tourist attraction.

It started with baseball cards when he was a kid growing up on a farm near Bruneau. Later, he collected old farm machinery. Then it was yard sales, estate sales, auctions...

"When nobody would bid, I'd bid a dollar," he said. "I liked bringing boxes of junk home and seeing what was in them. Sometimes there'd be an antique at the bottom."

In time, one man's junk became an Idaho treasure. It looks like the state's biggest yard sale. It fills building after building, spans more than a century of Americana. This spring, it opened to the public.

Lawson and his wife have turned farm buildings into a Western village and museum in the Owyhee County desert. Their nearest neighbors are scorpions. The nearest town is Oreana, population 25, and it's seven miles away.

"I had my doubts," he admits. "I thought, 'Who would come clear out here to see all this junk?' But they do."

The only advertising for the "Emu-z-um" — the name comes from their defunct emu business — is word-of-mouth. It seems to be enough.

"We built this for ourselves," Belva Lawson said, "but when the visitors center in Mountain Home found out about it, they went crazy. They brought a busload over, and people have been coming ever since. We've probably had close to 500."

Most of the bus's 44 passengers were "lifelong Idahoans who had no idea the place existed," center coordinator Jo Wright said. "They were amazed. We couldn't believe all the stuff that's out there in the middle of nowhere."

The stuff starts with the horse-drawn cultivators, binders and other farm machines lining the Lawsons' driveway — 84 of them.

They have a chuck wagon, sheep wagon, freight wagon, stagecoach, a pioneer cabin and replicas of an old-time barber shop and gas station, apple peelers, cherry pitters, lemon squeezers, cream separators.

They have a moonshine still. "This was Grampa Jack Pinard's still," Lawson said. "The stuff was about 110 proof. He had a bar over in Pine."

The Western village, formerly emu sheds, has a blacksmith's shop, sheriff's office, jail, saloon, assay office, post office, hotel, general store, school, church and cemetery. Many of its props are authentic pieces of Idaho's past.

The post office mail drop graced the post office in Grand View for more than 50 years. Students at the old Lake Lowell grade school used the faded wooden swing outside the village school. The hotel's ornately printed mirror came from the Keefer Hotel in Shoshone:

"Hot baths, 15 cents. Water changed weekly.

"Clean beds, 25 cents. Special group rate — up to six persons per bed. No horses permitted in rooms."

The village holds antiques from fence stretchers to pencil sharpeners. And the village is just the beginning.

"The problem with our tours is they're too long," Belva Lawson said. "One couple stayed 5-plus hours. Average is an hour and a half. We wear some people out. Right, Pa?"

They call each other Ma and Pa. Pa didn't answer. He was practically sprinting to the next tour stop.

"This is our old emu trailer," he said. "I'm not sure what to call it now."

One end of the trailer is the barber shop. A 10-cent Pepsi machine stands next to the barber's chair Belva Lawson's grandfather used for 60 years in Moscow and Grand View. The middle of the trailer is an old-fashioned kitchen and parlor. The other end is a bedroom. The black gown hanging beside the bed belonged to actress Ann Sothern.

The old barn is now a museum of farm memorabilia from milking machines to fly catchers. The old emu-feed building is the American Indian room. It's filled with artifacts and craftwork.

"This was one of my storage buildings," Lawson said at the next structure. "I showed Belva a picture of me as a kid at my dad's station in Bruneau, and look what happened."

What happened was a replica of Lawson's Utoco Station. A 1930 Ford is parked in the bay, next to a Flying A ethyl pump.

"Let's look in here," he said, opening the door of yet another building. "This used to be my shop, but Belva kicked me out."

Now it's a sports bar. Antique fishing tackle fills a crumbling wooden boat salvaged from a farmer's burn pile. An unopened bottle of Lucky Lager beer waits on a counter near the pinball machine.

The next building is crammed with so many kinds of things he can't decide what to call it — old newspapers, a hog scraper, corn shellers, a wooden propeller, wooden toys...

"These are toys of farm machines from the 1800s and early 1900s. Bob Wilson over in Grand View made them. You won't see these anywhere else because there ain't no more, and that's the absolute truth. We don't stretch a thing around here."

Belva's Disney collection — porcelain dolls, comic books, lunch pails, etc. — occupies a room of their rambling white farmhouse. Another room is brimming with old china, old clothes, Jack's mother's salt and pepper shaker collection, antique cake molds, antique egg scales...

"They have a cherry pitter that still works," recent visitor Yvonne Trippett said. "They seem to have everything. I used to teach fifth-grade history, and I was just fascinated. It would be a fabulous place to bring children, because they'd have fun and learn history at the same time."

Some of it's worth a lot of money — something they've never had.

"We're just broke old farmers," Jack said. "We've worked hard all our lives, raised two kids and never had any money. I wouldn't even try to figure up what all this stuff is worth.

"If you go by the antique value, it wouldn't have been possible. We got it because it was cheap. I'd buy it for a dollar a box or get it from scrap dealers for $40 a ton.

"A lot of it lately has been donated. Once people saw what we were doing, there was quite a response."

"We're old school," Belva added. "We figure if you charge more than a dollar a tour, it's too much. But we can't do it for that because the tours take so long. Even at $5, it just about pays for the paint and repairs."

At 59 — Belva is a year younger — Jack claims to be semi-retired. All he does is collect things, build and maintain the buildings, manicure the grounds, do tours and farm 420 acres of hay and pinto beans.

"It ain't no get-rich deal. But that's OK. We don't want to be rich. We're stay-at-home kind of people.

"We do this because we enjoy it, and because it's nice to preserve this stuff. Most everybody enjoys seeing it. They may have used it or remember it from when they were kids. There's a lot of wonderful memories in this old junk."

'Our little piece of heaven'
(Sept. 19, 2006)

BONE — In the Treasure Valley, where population growth sets annual records, a place like Bone seems almost unimaginable.

In booming Ada and Canyon counties, new businesses and housing developments seem to spring up overnight. Gridlock and red alerts are facts of life. The Valley's explosive growth has made Idaho the third-fastest growing state and Boise the Northwest's third-largest city.

For the exact opposite, go to Bone. Growth is virtually unknown in this southeastern Idaho hamlet, where population changes tend toward subtraction.

"The population used to fluctuate between two and five," Bone Store manager Sherry Day said. "It's been two for a few years now."

That, according to Alan Porter of the Idaho Department of Commerce and Labor, would likely make it the smallest town in Idaho.

Its "city center" is the rustic Bone Store, nestled in a hollow along a winding dirt road through rolling farmland. You can get anything from pickled eggs to a root beer float to a wine cooler at the store. Its ceiling is papered with dollar bills signed by customers, local cattle brands are burned into the woodwork and elk napkin dispensers line the lunch counter. The bench on the front deck is a chainsaw carving of a bone.

The store is open only Fridays and weekends; Day lives an hour away in Idaho Falls — or, in local parlance, "the Falls."

About 25 ranching families live in the hills around Bone, but most leave in the winter. The town's two actual residents live in a manufactured house across the road from the store, work in Idaho Falls and are home so seldom that neither Day nor area ranchers questioned knew their names.

Bone is so small and isolated it was the last town in Idaho to get phone service — in 1982. Dale Meyer, whose ranch is three miles up the road, remembers the first telephone conversation.

"My uncle, Gardner Johnson, called a lady named Blanche Beckwood," Meyer said. "They were both homesteaders. They talked for about five minutes about what it was like to have phones.

"Before the phones went in, we had to drive up a hill in our pickups and call out on CB radios."

Bone is named for homesteader Orion Yost Bone, who founded the original store in the early 1900s. It burned and was rebuilt in a slightly different location about 1945 to serve the local trade and people passing through.

"We get a lot of ranchers, stock truck drivers, fishermen and hunters; hardly anyone from the Falls," Day said. "They stop for a burger, our homemade pie or our old-fashioned root beer floats."

Or something stronger. Beer signs gleam in the front windows; coolers beckon with beverages from fuzzy navels to Smirnoff Twisted Watermelon. Deep in Mormon country — Bonneville County is 71 percent LDS — the store has a beer and wine license and does a brisk business in alcoholic beverages.

"You wouldn't think there'd be a lot of call for that here, but there is," Day said. "It's never been a bar, though, and I don't want it to be. I want it to stay a store and cafe."

Bone itself, however, may be on the cusp of change. Actor Vin Diesel is rumored to have built a home in the hills nearby. Subdivisions are contemplated.

"People used to say, 'Why would you want to live in Bone?'" Meyer said. "Now they say, 'Boy, it's nice around here; do you have a piece of ground you'd sell us?'

"I don't mind people coming in, but I like Bone better the way it's always been. It's our little piece of heaven."

The Old Hotel McCall
(Sept. 1, 1988)

MCCALL – The Hotel McCall, a landmark for half a century, is about to be "modernized."

The hotel, according to the Central Idaho Star-News, has been sold to a California woman who intends to "bring it up to modern-day safety standards and renovate its appearance."

That's good news for McCall. But to those who stayed at the old hotel under the management of its former owners, Lawrence and Blanche Luce, it's also kind of sad.

I never met Blanche Luce, but I met Lawrence, and I won't forget him. Luce is 91 now, but then he was just a kid in his early 80s. Someone had told me that staying at his hotel was like a visit to the 19th century, and as part of this column's continuing quest to seek out new experiences, I went to see for myself.

Anyone who has driven to McCall has seen this hotel – the white, three-story building on the right as you make the big left turn onto Main Street – but to have any idea of what it was like, you had to have stayed there. It was, literally, like no place else.

The first hint was check-in.

"That will be $11," the white-haired man at the desk said.

"I'm sorry. I thought you said $11."

"I did," he said, looking a bit put out.

It was too late to back out, so I paid and went upstairs to look for roaches. Any room that cost $11 a night had to have roaches.

The next hint was the room itself. No roaches anywhere. It was old, and definitely old-fashioned, but scrupulously maintained.

The one concession to the times was a television set big enough that, with wheels, it could have been used as a Soap Box Derby racer. On the table (doily, actually) next to the television were a box of chocolates, two bottles of fruit juice, a bucket of ice and two bottles of liquor.

Granted, they were the small, airline-sized bottles. But even so, the total cost had to have been around four dollars, or more than a third the price of the room.

That night, more surprises were waiting. While I was out for dinner, someone put another box of chocolates on the nightstand and turned down the bed.

No one had turned down my bed since I'd left home. I half expected to find a slice of Mom's apple pie on the table, but there was only a fresh bucket of ice. When you charge $11 for a room, you have to cut corners somewhere.

In the morning, a complimentary newspaper was waiting. Someone had pushed it under the door while I slept. This brought the value of the complimentary items to something approaching half the rate of the room. How could a hotel operate that way?

To find out, I went downstairs to ask the owner. (A local rumor – that when Luce took a liking to a customer he invited him into a back room for a nip of brandy – played no role in my decision.)

"We're Old World hotel people," he said, as if that explained everything. "This is the way we do things. Would you like some brandy?"

We sat in the back room for maybe half an hour while Luce told stories and talked about the hotel business. If anything, he was too good a host. My glass was never empty. A lot of businesses talk about personalized service; Luce really meant it.

The new owner of the Hotel McCall recently was quoted as saying that the upcoming renovation is intended to give the building "a little more personality."

They could start by hanging a picture in the lobby ... of the old owners.

The Peacock Woman
(June 12, 2004)

The Peacock Woman, Millie Norstebon.

ELMORE COUNTY — Millie Norstebon and her husband bought peacocks to try to control the rattlesnakes on their farm in a remote, desert canyon in Elmore County.

It worked. The rattlesnake population is half of what it was when they bought the birds 15 years ago.

The peacock population is something else, though.

"We started with two males and three hens," she said. "By last summer, we were up to about 60."

Peacocks strut in the yard and roost in the trees. They perch on fences, haystacks and rooftops and line the lava rock rim above Norstebon's home. Their haunting calls echo through the canyon. They seem to be everywhere.

If you want to know about peacocks, Millie Norstebon is the one to ask. She's sold peacocks to bird lovers throughout the valley and from Oregon, Washington and Nevada. She's known in four states as the peacock woman of Elmore County.

She's not in it for the money. Her price for the big birds with the beautiful feathers is only $20, and she's been known to give them away. Peahens — technically the word "peacock" refers only to males — produce up to a dozen chicks each spring. She sells the birds early in the winter, when they're about six months old, to keep the farm from being overrun by peacocks. But if she ever sold them all, which isn't likely, she'd miss them.

"I enjoy having them," she said. "I like watching them fan their feathers, and it's nice just to have them around the place and see them every day. They're beautiful, and they all have their own personalities."

Peacocks eat bread from her hand. When she works in her garden, they look over her shoulder to see what she's doing. When she mows the lawn, they follow her and eat the grass clippings.

Boisean Deb Gilbertson found the peacock woman through a classified ad after one of her daughters decided she wanted a peacock for Christmas.

"We came prepared to buy a pair," Gilbertson said. "When Millie saw that I had three girls, she asked her husband to give us a juvenile male as well. The kids were delighted."

Commonly thought of as sedate, strutting birds, peacocks are agile, aggressive, mobile. One of Norstebon's peacocks engages in daily combat with her turkeys. If the turkeys corner it, it erupts like a rocket on a launching pad and flies over them. Peacocks fly nightly from the rim of the canyon to the trees in her yard. She warns her customers to keep newly purchased birds penned up for a month, or they'll fly back to their former homes.

Gilbertson describes the peacock woman as "someone who has lived close to the land all her life, with an intense love for it. Weathered and tough, she could teach all of us a thing or two about self-sufficiency, as well as peafowl."

Now 68, Norstebon grew up on a farm in Minnesota. She and her husband, Stan, met and married there. He served all over the world as a mechanic in the Air Force. When the Air Force sent him to Mountain Home in 1970, they knew they'd found a home for life. He retired four years later, and they settled in rural Elmore County for good.

"It was just a nice quiet place in the country," she said. "You could go hunting and fishing and horseback riding, and it was a nice environment for raising children."

And animals. Their farm could almost be a game preserve. In addition to four children, they've raised cows, horses, dogs, cats, turkeys and peacocks. They feed quail and hummingbirds. The coyotes, owls, deer, raccoons, mink, bobcats, badgers, beavers and rattlesnakes that frequent the property are left to fend for themselves.

"When a snake comes around, five or six peacocks will get around it in a circle and peck it," Stan said. "They peck it so fast, it doesn't have a chance. I've never seen them eat one, but they definitely don't like them."

Their neighbor, Harold Doyle, has nine peacocks.

"I bought most of them from Millie," he said. "They're such a majestic bird. And they're good watchdogs, too. Anything out of the ordinary, and they scream like murder."

Their calls sound eerily like a woman screaming. Norstebon laughs as she tells a story about a man who went to check on a neighbor's wife, only to find that the alarming cries were coming from their peacocks.

Aggressive in defending their young (or feuding with turkeys), peacocks can be downright chummy with humans.

"If you're a stranger, they'll scream at you," Doyle said. "But they like being around people they know. Millie's follow her everywhere. Ours come up and sit on the porch with my wife while she has her coffee. They're very friendly. And believe it or not, they taste good, too."

Doyle barbecued two peacocks last summer. He plans to do the same this year.

Norstebon wouldn't think of eating a peacock, or even a peacock egg. She believes in maintaining a harmonious atmosphere on the farm.

"Everything's compatible around here," she said. "Until a peacock tries to eat out of the dog dish, and then there's trouble."

Their farm is what family farms used to be. They grow wheat and hay and raise a few head of cattle and horses. Stan works in the fields and the shop, Millie in the garden. The nearest "town" is Tipanuk, which is more a rural subdivision than a town. The Oregon Trail crosses their land; they can see the remnants of a stage stop from their yard. Old trees shade a lush lawn with an old-fashioned pump, a dinner bell, dozing dogs and preening peacocks.

"Mostly we just enjoy watching them," she said. "We have the chairs in the house arranged so we can watch the birds and the deer. We have it rough here."

One Man's Junk, Another's Bliss
(Sept. 10, 2005)

BLISS — Car after car passes Robert Grubbs's curious collection without stopping. Driver after driver assumes it's nothing but junk.

True, it doesn't look like much from the road — just another hodgepodge in yet another bypassed town. But Bob's Gifts and Rocks is an institution. The big dinosaur out front is a local landmark and the closest thing Bliss (population 275) has to a town symbol. And in the eyes of its owner, the piles of rocks, the faded dinosaur and the shop's shelves of assorted miscellany are things of beauty.

"Collecting rocks is my life," he says simply when asked to explain the appeal.

Rocks notwithstanding, calling his business a rock shop is like calling Wal-Mart a grocery store.

You can get a coffee cup, a lantern or a wagon wheel at Bob's.

A doll, a figurine, a fossil.

Need length of barbed wire? Bob's has it. A coil of telegraph wire? No problem.

"This is the wire that put the Pony Express out of business," he says, brandishing a strand of wire heavy enough to hold an elephant. "It was made to last."

You can get horseshoes and bridle hangers at Bob's. (A bridle hanger is a horseshoe welded to a railroad spike.)

Bottles in a bookcase gleam dully in the Indian Summer sun. He sells antique whiskey bottles, perfume bottles, wine bottles, medicine bottles, beer bottles, shoe-polish bottles...

"This is a boot bottle," he said, holding up a whiskey bottle dating back to the Wild West. "It was curved to fit around your leg so you could put it in your boot and still be comfortable."

Other shop offerings include rings, necklaces, pins, motor oil, carved onyx animals, telegraph regulators, marbles...

"Marbles are my biggest sellers. I'd starve without marbles. People who have never bought marbles in their lives will stop and pick out 30 at a time."

Hundreds of marbles sparkle in a bin in front of the shop. Grubbs prides himself on having reasonable prices, and the marbles are an example. They're priced at 30 for $1.

The most expensive item for sale at the moment is a 182-pound Moroccan marble sphere: $325.

The heaviest: a 750-pound hunk of crystallized quartz.

Grubbs's love affair with rocks began when he was a child growing up in Arkansas.

"I picked up my first rock in 1934," he said. "I think I still have it in the basement somewhere. But I didn't collect rocks very fast until two sisters told me their father had a lost mine. We went up there in August of '39, and it was like having your first cigarette or your first beer. I was hooked."

He came to Idaho in 1944, when his family migrated west, and after some moving around returned again in 1947. That was the year he bought one of the abandoned barracks buildings at the former Minidoka internment camp, moved it to Buhl and called it home. He attended the now-abandoned Normal school at Albion and later taught elementary school in Arkansas, Oregon, Deep Creek, near Buhl, and Dietrich, not far from Bliss.

He ran a laundry in Oklahoma, a mini-mart in Oregon and worked at a casino in Jackpot, Nev. But Bliss and rock collecting were never far from his mind. He owned a Bliss gift shop in the late '60s and early '70s — his late father made the dinosaur in 1970 out of plaster, old lumber and chicken wire — and after some moving around returned to Bliss for good in the 1980s.

"I opened up the shop on the Fourth of July and have been here ever since," he said. "I like it here because it's an easy way of life. There's no stress. Do you see anyone here who's hurrying?"

From his shop, it was a challenge to see anyone at all. When the Interstate bypassed Bliss 20 years ago, the town languished. Rising gas prices aren't helping.

"We used to see 10 cars at a time on the road through town," Grubbs said. "Now you have to wait sometimes to see one. We're not seeing anyone from east of the Mississippi now."

It's a quiet life. He's 77, a father of three and lives alone. Asked if his wife had passed away, he replied. "Yes. She's passed away to California. We were married for 20 years."

Home is some rooms behind the shop, where the only sound can be the unrelenting desert wind. The wind and the winters are the only things he doesn't like about Bliss.

"I get tired of the wind, and in the winter I can't get anything done," he said. "It takes two hours just to get the snow off of all my rocks."

White-haired, partial to slacks, sport shirts and cardigan sweaters, he looks like the snowbird he's become. In the fall, he packs up and drives to Quartzsite, Ariz., for the winter. He sells rocks there, too.

He has no idea how many kinds of rocks he has.

"There's no limit," he said. "There are rocks that haven't been discovered yet."

He collects what he can in the desert around Bliss, and suppliers ship him rocks from Mexico, Brazil, China, Morocco, India and Pakistan. He has thundereggs, dyed geodes, sliced jasper. He has rock eggs, rock urns, rock pyramids, rock bowls, rock book ends...

His rock-ribbed enthusiasm is contagious. Former Boisean David Munson, now of Kalispell, Mont., credits Grubbs with getting him and his wife into the rock business.

"He encouraged us to do what we love and helped get us started," Munson said. "I'd been haunting his shop since the 1980s because he's fun to talk to and has a multitude of things you can't get anywhere else. That big (750-pound) crystal is amazing. It should be in the Museum of Natural History.

"Bob knows everybody in the business and has a heart of gold. He doesn't price things where they belong. He sells them almost at his cost."

When he's not around, the shop operates on the honor system. A sign by the marbles tells prospective customers to help themselves and push the payment through a slot in the door.

He admits he's had "a little theft. But every time I'm gone, there's money waiting when I get back."

Neighbor Roy Mays says "you'd have to go a long ways to find another Bob. He's a good ol' boy. He's willing to help people any way he can. He goes out of his way to help people."

Those he's helped include an elderly couple in the Bruneau area.

"They can't get around much anymore," Munson said. "Bob makes sure they have clothes and enough to eat."

Money for himself isn't a high priority.

"I've never had any money in my whole life," the man who loves rocks said. "I get Social Security, but I'd be hungry if I didn't have this shop. The shop, the rocks — they're what keep me going. Without them, I don't know what I'd do."

Dinosaurs Can Be Anywhere
(Aug. 23, 2009)

HAGERMAN — Most people with a yard as big as Kenny Crist's would have trouble keeping it mowed. He turned his into a dinosaur park.

If Crist Dinosaur Park were a tourist attraction, it would be one of the more unusual ones around — dinosaur replicas, a one-hole golf course, a fishing pond filled with sturgeon

But it isn't a tourist attraction, at least not yet.

"It's just outside Hagerman, and people who live in Hagerman don't know it's there," Mario Delisio said. "I asked the Hagerman Chamber of Commerce, and they didn't even know about it."

Delisio, a Boisean, discovered the park in his travels as a tour-group leader. Like many visitors, he was struck by its eclectic beauty.

A concrete brontosaurus, a miniature Easter Island statue and a T-rex and cow made of discarded farm-machinery parts beckon from a rocky hillside. They aren't huge — the T-rex is 9 feet tall — but they're so odd and unexpected that they stop traffic — what little there is of it.

Scientifically, the location makes sense.

"The Hagerman Fossil Beds National Monument is right across the river," Crist said, "so I decided I'd build some dinosaurs."

The dinosaurs overlook a rolling lawn shaded by elm trees and dotted with park paraphernalia from picnic tables to an ancient teeter-totter. The

Crists have reserved it for weddings, reunions and other functions, free of charge.

"Two elderly women stopped for a picnic one day and asked who I was," Crist said. "They were surprised when I said I was the owner. They thought it was a public park."

A short walk from the picnic area, the spring-fed fishing pond is filled with trout, koi, blue gills, catfish, bass, crappie and other fish in addition to sturgeon.

"The biggest sturgeon is 6 feet 4 inches long and takes up to an hour to catch on 10-pound test line," Crist said. "I don't allow heavy line. I take reservations to fish here, but I've never charged anybody. I let people take fish home, but not the sturgeons. They're my pals."

The one-hole golf course is a recent addition.

"My son's a golfer, and I'm going to be."

Crist, 59, apologizes for the course not being in better shape and other projects not being finished. He and his two sons run a construction company and a tree service, so he doesn't have the time he'd like to spend on the dinosaur park.

The park started 20 years ago, when the Crists needed more room for gatherings and cleared some pasture for a picnic area. Kenny's father-in-law, Gene Padgett, was born there. Now 77, he's lived his whole life there.

"I spent thousands of hours working this land," he said. "It used to be isolated. Now we have neighbors."

Crist and his wife, Ronda, have spent the last 36 years there. They hope to have all of their projects, including eight more dinosaurs and a landscaped beach and pontoon-boat dock on the Snake River, finished in two years.

Their son and other relatives also live at the park. Their granddaughter Brianne, 12, likes to ride motorcycles and the brontosaurus (which has a saddle). She calls the park, "a wonderful place to grow up."

The "long-term plan is to just stay home and run things when we retire," Crist said. "We'd probably have to charge people then, but for now it's mostly just for people who know us and call ahead. I'm particular about who comes here."

He makes a point of finishing work early so he can spend time in his park.

"I just love being here," he said. "People say somebody will offer me the right amount of money to sell this place someday. There is no right amount."

For Serious Eaters Only
(Dec. 1, 1981)

Betty Sherrill scratched her chin, leaned against the cigarette-burned counter at Manley's Café, and thought it over.

"It's so hard to separate what's true from what's not true," she said. "They said Robert Kennedy ate here once, and the other one, too. The president, John Kennedy. For a dump, this place is pretty well known."

Manley's is no dump. It's a legend. Among eaters, Manley's Café is known, and loved, far beyond the borders of Idaho. Manley's is to prime rib and pie a la mode what Idaho is to potatoes. Clint Eastwood has eaten at Manley's. Arnold Palmer came here after hours and made his chauffer con the management into opening the place back up for one more piece of pie. Shields and Yarnel, the comedians, have eaten at Manley's. Eugene Fodor, the famous violinist, eats at Manley's. Without that plain little café on Federal Way, he might not have performed in Idaho.

"We get people in here from all over," Jan Barker said from her spot behind the cash register. "New York, Canada, a lot from California. The farthest anyone has come from was either Austria or Germany, I'm not sure which. He'd heard about it from an American who was traveling over there, and he said he wanted me to know he'd come all that way to eat here. My mouth dropped a foot."

Jan and Betty are the café's co-managers. They and their husbands bought it in 1978 from David Morrow, son of the original Manley. Manley died in 1977, but his philosophy sustains the business he began as Manley's Rose Garden almost 30 years ago. By philosophy, I mean food.

You don't go to Manley's any old time. You go there when you're hungry. Blue-ribbon hungry. If there is a place that serves larger meals, I haven't heard of it. Nothing fancy – just plain, good food and plenty of it. If you're a gourmet, go downtown. If you're famished, go to Manley's.

Order the prime rib. It costs $12.75 (the price just went up), but it weighs almost two pounds. Just seeing it on a plate is an experience the serious eater remembers for life. A larger version costs an extra $3.25 and comes on two plates. The management says it's more than enough for two people.

If you make it through the main course, try the pie a la mode. Betty gets up early and makes all the pies herself, from scratch. They're the old-fashioned kind; the big, thick ones in the deep pans. Each serving is a fifth of a pie. Around and on top of the pie is almost a quart of ice cream.

The serving of a Manley pie a la mode is forever an occasion. No matter how many times they've seen it happen, the customers ooh and aah as each slice is brought to the counter. On a recent Saturday evening, they oohed and aahed as a boy of about 12 squared off with a plate of blackberry a la mode. Bets were made. The smart money was on the pie, of course. The boy tried – no one could say he didn't – but it was soon obvious that he didn't have a chance. It was just too much pie.

My wife and I split a slice of blackberry a la mode for dessert and had trouble getting through it all. Our daughters, the pie monsters, split a slice of cherry, without ice cream, and left half of it on their plates. We gaped as the waitress presented the man next to us with a side of beef and a bushel of French fries.

"They've got to be kidding," he groaned. "Nobody could eat all this."

The waitress smiled and refilled his coffee without comment. She had heard it before; more times than she could remember. Manley's customers share their astonishment. It's the one thing they have in common.

On a good day, the customers eat 30 pies, 120 pounds of beef, and 15 gallons of ice cream. For larger eateries, with commodious booths and acres of tables, this wouldn't be impressive. But Manley's is just a little place – smaller than most people's houses. Most of it is kitchen. It has 24 stools, no booths, no tables. A single row of bare bulbs lights the knotty pine dining area. Outside, behind the removable "open" sign, is another sign. Hand-painted letters, red on white, "Gone fishin'."

"Manley was famous for closing," Betty said. "He was a nice guy and a good chef. We'll never change his concept of food – large meals and everything made from scratch – but when he got tired he just quit working. He'd put up the gone fishin' sign and close it up for a month."

I talked with Jan and Betty for half an hour or so, enough time for the customer on my left to consume a small herd of cattle. Neither co-manager realized it until I told them, but they once served one of the most famous eaters of all.

A couple of years ago, Calvin Trillin came to Idaho to research one of his U.S. Journal pieces for the New Yorker. Trillin, as any devoted eater knows, is the author of numerous food articles and two food books, "Kentucky Fried," and "Alice, Let's Eat." He also is a regular on The Tonight Show, where he is apt to talk about anything from Kansas City barbecue to the Guadalajara chili cook-offs.

Where do you take such a man for lunch?

We took him to Manley's. He thanked us three times.

Murray's Girls
(Oct. 16, 1994)

Just a little knockabout place, but it's funny how it brought so many people together. – Fannie Flagg, "Fried Green Tomatoes."

The circle of women enjoying the sunshine on The Grove could have been a bridge group or a gardening club.

They sat on benches, sharing stories and sack lunches. Ten women, middle-aged or better, clearly enjoying themselves. Peals of laughter peppered the conversation.

Once they were May queens, girls who turned heads. Now the hair is graying; the roses in the cheeks have dimmed. The memories haven't.

"Remember the initiations?" one of them asks. "Remember how we'd take the new kids down in the basement and roll them in sawdust."

Laughter.

"Remember Tim?"

"The fountain boy?"

"Ooh, yes! The good-looking one. He was dreamy!"

Sighs.

"Have you seen our brick yet?"

They walk across The Grove, stopping on the edge of a circle of engraved bricks.

"Here it is. Let's take a picture."

They gather round the brick, which is inscribed with the name of their common bond: Murray's Curb Service.

A recent subject of this column, the Murray's building at 8th and Broad is to be torn down to make way for a parking lot. The women wanted to meet one last time at the place that brought them all together, then as carhops, now as companions in the court of memory.

"I think people were politer then."

"They were. They had more respect for each other. In all those years, I don't think we had trouble with a customer more than once or twice."

One of the women worked at Murray's 25 years. Another was there 27 years, from the '40s until the drive-in closed in '72.

They spoke affectionately of "Mr. Murray," whose heart was made of gold but had walls of paper. Toward the end, when it was killing him, they'd find him lying in his car, too sick to come inside and work.

They reminisced about Hazel Johns, who with her husband ran Murray's during the '50s and '60s. The heart of the business for 20 years, she helped carhops pay college tuition, shared her home with them, held their sore paws when they were feeling low.

In the late '80s, Hazel had a stroke and returned to the best days of her life, the Murray's days. Relatives would find her fumbling with keys on her porch at dawn, thinking she was opening the restaurant for business. Or giving orders in her kitchen, calling out the names of long-departed cooks and waitresses.

From The Grove, the women walk up 8th Street to their former haunt, now a vacant furniture store. At the corner of 8th and Broad, they stop to have their picture taken under an enormous sycamore tree.

"It was just a sapling when we worked here. We had to water it every night."

"Remember the girl who got the night off by calling in and saying her cow fell in the well?"

Laughter.

"Mr. Murray made her a trophy. He said it was the best excuse he'd ever heard."

More laughter.

"Those were good times."

"You said it."

A memorial is planned. By spring, a plaque will mark the spot that brought them together and that will live on in their hearts. It will be under the sycamore tree, the one the car hops had to water every night.

A Simpler Time and Place
(June 20, 2010)

Before Boise was "discovered," before it was even a metro area, a big star came to town and wove a spell.

The star was Clint Eastwood. The spell was "Bronco Billy," an Eastwood film that premiered in Boise 30 years ago this month.

No one who lived here then will forget Bronco Billy and his Wild West Show. Especially the hundreds of Treasure Valley residents who were extras or had bit parts in the movie that was shot at many locations in the Valley.

"It was Big Hollywood coming to a little town," Linda Hironimus said. "They expected the Hollywood people to be snooty, but they were just the opposite. Especially Eastwood. He was kind and gentle to everyone. It was like a big family."

Hironimus is editor and co-publisher of a limited-edition book about the making of "Bronco Billy." Written by Nampan Sandy Kershner and due early next month, it will be sold at the Canyon County Historical Museum as a museum fundraiser.

Kershner spent three years researching and writing "On the Trail with Bronco Billy." She went to dozens of the Valley locations where it was made, and she interviewed as many locals as she could who were in the film.

"Everyone I talked to had good things to say about Eastwood," she said. "He made a wonderful impression because he and his crew were so friendly to everyone."

An example: One scene was filmed near the Elks Rehabilitation Hospital, where a 14-year-old patient was close to dying. Brenda Krueger, then an occupational therapist there, knew the teen was an Eastwood fan. So Krueger walked across the street, through security and told the big star about the sick kid who would love to meet him. Eastwood dropped everything and left the set.

"He visited with her at her bedside and kissed her hand," Krueger said. "It was really quite sweet."

The girl said she'd never wash her hand again. And meant it.

Lots of kids skipped all or part of a day of school to watch the filming. Eastwood thanked them for their interest, then gently lectured them for missing school.

Just like Bronco Billy would have done.

For those who never saw it, Bronco Billy was a different kind of role for Eastwood the tough guy. Bronco Billy was an idealist who strove to be a positive role model for "the little buckaroos." Eastwood called him "a last holdout against cynicism in our society today."

The story was based on the life of Dennis Hackin, its author.

"His parents were city slickers, but they always wanted to be a cowboy and cowgirl so they bought a farm in Arizona," Hironimus said. "They taught their kids to do their chores, be honest and kind to others, say their prayers at night and have good values."

Just like Bronco Billy.

"Bronco Billy" isn't Eastwood's best film, but it did have a certain, well, sweetness. And here it was a local phenomenon. Kershner estimates that 2,000 Idahoans were in it. Boiseans Pam Abbas, Doug Copsey, Mike Reinbold and Roger Simmons were among those with speaking roles. The rest of us were extras.

I was in a carnival scene, running after one of my daughters. She and my wife were in an audience scene.

Oddly, the person I associate most closely with Eastwood during the filming had nothing to do with it. Candy Loving, Playboy's 25th anniversary "Playmate," was here on a tour, and I had an assignment to spend a day with her for a story. We went to a party where Eastwood showed up unexpectedly, and someone suggested that they climb into a heart-shaped tub, fully clothed, for a photo.

He'd been filming all day and looked dead tired, but he did it. In fact, he couldn't have been nicer about it. Maybe there really was a bit of Bronco Billy in him.

Or maybe, as Hironimus put it, it was just a simpler time and place.

"All towns grow up, including Boise," she said. "But then it was innocent. It was the kind of place where Bronco Billy really could ride through town and bond with people. It was special. There was something almost magical about it."

Idaho-Iowa
(March 26, 2007)

Idaho-Iowa madness is back. Actually, it never left.

Longtime readers may recall an irregular series of columns I did on the confusion between the two states. Mix-ups happened often enough that I collected enough material for a small book about it:

There was the air-freight pilot who successfully bid for his company's Boise assignment because he thought Boise was a bedroom community of Des Moines. The last I heard, he was still living here.

The Idaho Falcons soccer team traveled to a tournament in Russia, where a group of locals adopted them because they had no fans of their own. The Russians graciously made them a banner, which they proudly taped to the Idahoans' tour bus.

The banner's message: "Go, Iowa."

Harper's Magazine ran the first correction in its history after identifying an Idaho congressman as an Iowa Republican.

The Wall Street Journal moved Sun Valley to Iowa.

Tom Brokaw once ended a piece with the deliciously satisfying, "This is Tom Brokaw, reporting from Boise, Iowa."

Even the White House mis-addressed a letter to Pocatello, Iowa.

I've given the Idaho-Iowa confusion a long rest — a book of it seemed to be enough — but recent events compel its resurrection. One was an e-mail from a former Statesman editor, now of Des Moines, containing the following item from Editor and Publisher, a trade journal:

"Todd Dvorak has been named correspondent in charge of the Associated Press' Boise, Iowa bureau. Previously, Dvorak was AP's Iowa City correspondent.

The story's headline: "Todd Dvorak to Head AP Bureau in Boise, Iowa."

The masterstroke, the one that convinced me to reprise the Idaho-Iowa segments, was a story in the Honolulu Advertiser. My story, actually. The Honolulu paper reprinted a story I'd written on development of wind energy in Idaho. It was faithfully reproduced with repeated references to Idaho and Idaho towns, including Bone, Albion, Hagerman, Nampa and Boise.

The Advertiser's banner headline: "A mighty wind blowing in Iowa's future."

When they start screwing up my own stories with Iowa headlines, it's time to fight back.

It Never Ends
(April 16, 2007)

Jim Franklin was right. Franklin was a geography teacher I knew who couldn't get a job teaching the subject he loved. He'd taught at the university level, but demand for geography teachers had fallen so much that the last time I saw him he was selling suits at Penney's.

He feared that we were approaching the point of geographic illiteracy, and the response to a column of mine last month on Idaho-Iowa mix-ups has proved him right. Far from subsiding since I'd last written about it more than a decade earlier, the confusion appears to have intensified.

If the University of Idaho's experience with guest lecturers is an indication, even great legal minds are geographically challenged.

Boisean Jill Twedt e-mailed about a gaffe by U.S. Supreme Court Justice Antonin Scalia, who spoke in Moscow as part of the university's Bellwood Lecture Series.

"Standing in front of the largest University of Idaho banner, Justice Scalia proclaimed that it was his pleasure to have been invited to speak at the University of Iowa," Twedt wrote.

That was in 2000. Five years later, Minnesota Supreme Court Justice and Pro Football Hall of Fame member Alan Page stepped in the same sinkhole.

"As he began his remarks, for which the university had paid him handsomely, he said that it was very good to be here in Iowa," Ritchie

Eppink e-mailed. "He corrected himself a sentence or two later, but not before the eye-rolling and forehead-holding had begun."

Former Boisean Matthew Cordell, now of Phoenix, wondered why a co-worker continually asked him how his Idaho parents were faring during a flood on the Mississippi River.

"The last time she asked me, I told her rather forcefully that they were in Idaho, not Iowa," he wrote. "'Oh, I know that,' she said. 'I just thought that maybe the flood waters had backed up to where they live.'"

Of course. Right after they flooded Montana.

Cordell, who has lived in Phoenix since 1979, says he's given up on trying to explain where Idaho is:

"Most of the confusion involves Iowa, even if it isn't expressed... I told a man from New York that I was from the Northwest so I wouldn't have to explain the Idaho thing. It didn't work."

"Seattle?" the New Yorker wanted to know. "Portland?"

"No," Cordell replied. "Idaho. The Boise area."

"You call that the Northwest? Boise's in the Midwest."

Right. Just up the road from Sioux City.

Boisean Christine Bauer received a voice-mail recently from a man who said he was looking for a long-lost relative in "Des Moines, Idaho."

"I don't know if I would have embarrassed him by correcting him," she said, "or would he just have been more confused?"

Irene Schmidt called to say that her parents once received an ill-timed letter telling them that relatives from Caldwell were planning to visit them. Her parents were living in Des Moines, Wash., at the time. (There really is such a place.) A postal employee crossed out Washington and replaced it with Iowa. The letter arrived a week after the visit was over.

When he was a college student in Ohio, Boisean Bob Olson went to a Western Union office there to send a telegram to Aberdeen, Idaho.

"What big town is that near?" the Western Union agent asked him.

"Pocatello," Olson replied.

The agent thumbed through his book, frowned and asked, "How far's that from Des Moines?"

Answer: A thousand miles, give or take.

Though Idaho and Iowa are the most commonly confused states, they certainly aren't the only ones. When Jef Gleason informed his relatives in the East that he was moving to Boise, they asked him how far it was from Columbus.

Gleason has made up his own name for the state of confusion: "Idahohiowa."

Colleen Maile received a letter last month addressed to her in "Eagle, Indiana 83616."

"At least they got the zip code right," she said.

For multi-state muddles, however, it's hard to beat the letter sent to Jim Toomey at "The University of Idaho, Iowa City, Ohio."

That Toomey actually received the letter is a tribute to a too-often maligned segment of our work force. Whatever they're paying postal workers to make sense of our geographic mayhem, it's a bargain.

The Face of Teton
(June 9, 1996)

The Teton Dam disaster left countless images, but none more haunting than the face of Anna Ballard.

When the dam burst 20 years ago last week, I was part of the international army sent to cover the disaster of the century in Idaho.

The Kellogg mining disaster claimed more lives but disrupted fewer. And it had nothing of the staggering devastation left by Teton, the flood that might as well have been a bomb.

The view from the airplane as we landed was numbing. A good portion of eastern Idaho seemed to be under water. Homes and other buildings had literally exploded. Entire towns had vanished. It's impossible not to be awed by that kind of power.

Ricks College, on high ground overlooking flooded Rexburg, looked like an outsized rescue mission. More than 2,000 victims, suddenly homeless, wandered the campus in hopes of obtaining food and shelter. These were people who had lost everything. No one who was there will forget the dazed expressions of disbelief.

I spoke with an obscure faculty member who said that if it wasn't for Ricks, "things would be in one hell of a mess here." His name was Richard Stallings. Confined to campus, the future congressman had yet to comprehend the disaster's magnitude. Eleven dead and a billion dollars in property damage is, with due respect, one hell of a mess.

Stallings had a point, though. The college and the Mormon Church helped thousands. The church is known for taking care of its own, and, in Southeast Idaho, that includes just about everybody.

But not Anna Ballard.

I met her at what had been her home in Roberts, about 30 miles from the dam. Her secondhand mobile home was twisted like a corkscrew. Everything she owned was gone.

Anna wasn't a Mormon. She had no fellow church members to lean on and little cause for hope. She wasn't young; her husband's salary was less than $3,000 a year; and the flood had washed away his job and any realistic chance of finding another.

It's impossible to describe the stricken expression on her face, her eyes luminous with tears as she struggled to comprehend her loss. For me, that was the face of the Teton Dam disaster. A face of consummate devastation.

I tried to find her last week, but it was as if the tide had carried her away. No Ballards were listed, and no one I spoke with could remember anything about her.

Could it happen again?

In another part of the state last month, I stood deep inside a high dam with torrents of water leaking from eroding bedrock through tons of concrete. It was scary.

The people in charge say it's safe.

They say the same thing about Lucky Peak, and, to date, the evidence suggests they're right.

They said Teton was safe, too.

After it burst, there was a movement to rebuild the dam. In a fit of good sense, it failed.

The great dam-building era, which spanned much of this century, has about spent itself. Most of the suitable sites, as well as some unsuitable ones, have been developed.

Occasionally, just often enough to provide a modicum of hope, we learn from our mistakes.

Leave Malad Gorge Alone!
(Dec. 4, 1990)

Now it's Malad Gorge.

You'd think some of nature's creations would be so awe-inspiring, so obviously public treasures, that no one would want to compromise them for profit.

You would, that is, if you hadn't seen it happen time and time again.

When I was a rookie reporter, the battle was over protecting the Sawtooth and White Cloud mountains. How anyone with a shred of sensitivity could look at those mountains and not think they needed protection defies comprehension, but never underestimate the power of a dollar.

A few years ago, it was Upper Mesa Falls, one of the state's least-discovered and most spectacular treasures. No less an authority than Wallace Stegner described them as "purity absolute." To visit Upper Mesa Falls, he wrote, is to "refuse to believe that you will ever be tired or old."

Unless there's a hydro plant humming in your ears.

That brings us to Malad Gorge – Idaho's latest candidate for hydroelectric power.

Perhaps you've never seen Malad Gorge. Relatively few Idahoans have, though they may have passed over it countless times without knowing it. The gorge is a paradox – one of Idaho's most breathtaking sights, and one of its most overlooked.

To get there, take Interstate 84 to the Tuttle exit, two hours east of Boise. A freeway bridge crosses a narrow section of the gorge, but the traffic flashes over it so quickly that most travelers aren't aware of its presence. If they were, they wouldn't be so quick to dismiss southern Idaho as a scenic wasteland.

The few who take the exit and follow the signs to Malad Gorge State Park are rewarded with a view of one of the scenic wonders of this or any state.

From the desert floor, the canyon drops 250 feet. Straight down. One step and you're on solid ground; the next you're a footnote on a warning sign.

A walking bridge crosses the gorge above a cataract called the Devil's Washbowl. From there, it is possible to experience the abyss in all its heart-stopping immensity – the sun glinting off the lava rock, the canyon walls changing colors in the shifting light, the jade river, the swallows riding the air currents. …

But I'm trying to describe the indescribable.

Last summer, having threatened for several years to take my children there, I made the gorge the first stop on a family reunion trip to the Midwest. I expected them to take one look and ask how far it was to the nearest McDonald's, but they were in awe of the place.

We stayed nearly an hour, admiring the scenery and wildlife and oohing and aahing as tumbleweeds thrown from the bridge sailed hundreds of yards on the summer wind. Three weeks and 5,000 miles later, I asked the kids their favorite part of the vacation.

"Wrigley Field," came the response, "and that place with the beavers and the tumbleweeds."

It would be nice to think that children of the future could experience the gorge's grandeur, undeveloped and uncompromised.

One of its prospective developers said that if he thought a hydroelectric plant would harm the gorge, he'd be against it.

That's a little like a fox saying that if a doggy door would harm the chicken house, he'd be against it.

The Malad Gorge is one of Idaho's natural treasures.

Leave it the way it is.

North Fork Fiasco
(Jan. 19, 1988)

If someone wanted to use one of the Sawtooth Mountains to make gravel for highways in the state of Washington, the people of Idaho would be ready to go to war.

So why is it that when someone tries to turn one of the state's most scenic rivers into puddles to make power for (among other places) the city of Tacoma, Wash., the average Idahoan remains silent?

As reported in Sunday's Statesman, power brokers in Idaho and Washington are continuing negotiations over the technicalities of building a $300 million hydroelectric project on the North Fork of the Payette River.

Power produced by the project would be used by the city of Tacoma and sold to utilities in the Southwest.

The part of the North Fork that is being studied is the stretch between Banks and Smiths Ferry, the part that makes your heart beat faster as you drive Idaho 55 toward Cascade.

One point should be made early on. Spectacular as it is, the North Fork is not a pristine example of nature's handiwork. Without Cascade Dam, the river during much of the summer would be a trickle, and some of the white water is the result of the stream's tumbling over rocks blasted from canyon walls during construction of the highway and the Idaho Northern railroad tracks.

"It didn't have any flow of any size in late July and August until Cascade Dam was built in the late 1940s," Idaho Public Utilities Commissioner Perry Swisher said. "Cascade is a very shallow reservoir which is open to the sun, so it gets the water up to about 70 degrees and dumps it onto rocks pushed into the canyon by the railroad and the highway department, and this is their pristine stream. It's actually more like Disneyland."

None of which makes it any less beautiful. In fact, the North Fork is one of a relatively few cases in which the work of men actually has enhanced the work of nature.

Years ago, I met a seasoned river guide who said it made him sweat just to drive by the North Fork. He didn't know that it wasn't as nature created it. If he had, it probably wouldn't have mattered. Like countless other observers, he was awed by its power and beauty, regardless of their sources.

In his 1982 guidebook, "Idaho for the Curious," Cort Conley describes the stream as "a smoky white turmoil of haystacks and souse holes – it drops 1,700 feet in 15 miles."

Forty-five years earlier, in another Idaho guide, Vardis Fisher wrote that "in springtime (the North Fork) rolls furiously in white cascades with few interruptions, with dense evergreen growth carpeting the walls down to its edge."

What guidebook could fail to mention such an attraction? For generations of Idahoans and visitors alike, the river has been a sightseer's delight.

Some of my earliest memories of traveling in Idaho are of stopping beside the roaring water during weekend trips to McCall with relatives. Often as not, we were accompanied by friends or distant relatives, who were visiting from out-of-state, and the roadside turnouts provided ideal opportunities to impress them.

"One of the longest stretches of white water in the world!" someone would say every time.

The guests invariably would marvel. I never did know whether the claim was true, but if nothing else it demonstrated the pride that people took in the spectacle.

If the hydroelectric project is built as planned, Swisher said, the river "would be smaller. From July through October, it wouldn't be very white."

You have to wonder about the priorities of people who would do that to a scenic attraction acclaimed far beyond our borders.

The North Fork is part of what makes Idaho special. It should stay the way it is.

National Park? Forget it.
(Feb. 26, 1987)

You have to hand it to Larry Craig.

When it comes to off-the-wall ideas, Idaho's First District congressman makes the inventor of the Edsel look like an amateur.

Craig, you may recall, is the one who wanted to build a highway across the Frank Church-River of No Return Wilderness. Later, after learning that the majority of Idahoans found the plan slightly less popular than gun control, he said he wasn't serious.

Everyone knows what a cutup he is.

Now Craig wants to turn the White Cloud and Sawtooth Mountains into a national park.

"The potential economic benefits to Idaho are obvious," he said. "Yellowstone and Grand Teton national parks are right next door, and they're bursting at the seams."

That's just what Idaho needs, all right. To take two of the most exquisite parts of the state, areas generations of Idahoans have treasured for their beauty and solitude, and turn them into places "bursting at the seams" with people would be irresponsible even for Craig.

Of course, it's hard to tell when he's being serious and when he's joking. Maybe this is just another case of the congressman regaling the populace with his legendary wit.

Fifteen years ago, I had the opportunity to see what happens to a place that is being considered for national-park status. By coincidence, it was much of the same area that lately had fallen under the eye of Rep. Craig. But I'm getting ahead of my story. For the proper background, it is necessary to go back five more years, to the summer of 1967.

That was the summer that the U.S. Navy in Pensacola, Fla., decided it couldn't get along without me. As a prelude to my demise, a friend and I decided to go fishing in the Sawtooth Mountains. Our destination was a lake that in those days was, if not inaccessible, at least somewhat remote. It took seven hours to hike there, although five would have been sufficient under normal conditions. (By normal conditions, I mean the absence of my friend's backpack, which weighed 90 pounds and had an iron skillet dangling from it, banging on the rocks.)

We stayed four days. The fishing was disappointing, as it often is at high mountain lakes, but the experience was unforgettable. It was enough just to be in such a place, where everything was as it always had been and nothing had been lessened by the grasping hand of man. We didn't need signs or rangers to remind us not to mess it up. The reminders were everywhere.

In four days during the height of the summer tourist season, we didn't see another soul, or even any signs of people. No debris, no campfires other than our own, not even a footprint.

Five years later, what a difference!

Returning to share the lake's unspoiled beauty with some newly acquired in-laws, I was surprised to find the lot at the trailhead jammed with cars. We were lucky to get the last parking place. All of the cars but ours had out-of-state license plates.

"This is the trail to the lake with no people?" one of the relatives incredulously asked.

"I'll bet all this is because of that Sunset article," his wife replied.

There is nothing new about Craig's proposal; the area was being considered for national-park status then, too. The idea was wisely rejected, but Sunset, in typical, cheerleading style, had just done a glowing piece on "the Sawtooths, America's newest national park."

Several of the cars in the parking lot had copies of the magazine on their seats or dashboards.

Where there had been no one just a few years before, there were crowds. The solitude had given way to an unending procession of manmade sights and sounds. Worst was the garbage. Where we hadn't seen so much as a footprint on the previous trip, the trail was strewn with candy wrappers, cigarette packages, broken whiskey bottles.

At the lake, it was worse. People had scrawled their initials on rocks, carved them into trees. Young trees had been pulled from the ground and thrown into fires. Campsites were littered with paper plates, empty cans and other junk. A college student had been hired to enforce campground regulations, clean up the trash, and, presumably, direct traffic.

How anyone could have such little regard for such heart-stopping beauty is beyond me, but it happens. If there is one thing the experience taught me (and it's something Rep. Craig would do well to consider), it was never to underestimate people's capacity to ruin the places they love.

Eight or nine years later, I went back to the lake with some friends. National park fever had long since subsided, and a measure of the old tranquility had returned.

No one is saying that Idaho's beauty should be locked up for a few. It belongs to all Americans.

But that doesn't mean it should be exploited until it's "bursting at the seams" in the name of economic progress.

Only an opportunist would say that.

A Good Place to Call Home
(July 1, 1990)

Most pioneer families came to Idaho for economic reasons. Mine came for the sun.

Bert Woodward, my father, was a salesman. He spent the 1930s in Portland and Seattle, working for the Procter & Gamble Co. and waiting for the sun to shine.

It didn't.

"He kept waiting and waiting and waiting, but it rained every day," my mother recalled. "One dreary morning he got up and decided he'd had it. He packed his suitcases, called the company and said he was going where the sun shone. When he got to Idaho, it was sunny. He fell in love with it and stayed the rest of his life."

Our Idaho pioneers, the ones who make me a fifth- instead of a second-generation Idahoan, were on her side of the family. Their reasons for coming here are less clear.

My maternal great-great-grandfather, Aaron McCoy, moved the clan from Iowa to California in a covered wagon after the Civil War. Things didn't work out in California, so he came to the Northwest, stopping his wagon for the last time at Lewiston.

Why he stayed there is something of a mystery – my guess is his horses took one look at the Lewiston grade and threw in the sponge – but there things did work out for him. A minister-farmer, he raised crops, ran a Protestant church, made friends. Anyone who came to church was welcome at his home for Sunday dinner.

Why do the rest of us continue to stay? Well, I can't speak for all of the tribe, but speaking for myself …

At the bottom of it all, I suppose, is that Idaho is a good place to live. That sounds awfully obvious, but it involves a combination of factors that doesn't exist in quite the same way anyplace else.

Boise is one of a very few places where you can see wild geese, blue heron, horse pastures, cowboys, trout fishermen, mounted policemen, a university, performing arts center, pavilion, state capitol and corporate world headquarters buildings, all on your way to work in the morning.

I know because I see most of those things on my way to work every week.

From my house, I can see mountains that look close enough to touch. (Mountains are a big part of Idaho – and Idahoans. No true Idahoan can be entirely content away from them.) A five-minute walk takes me to a quiet glade by a sparkling river. Mallard ducks land in my yard.

Boise is the only place I know where, in the same day, you can see a Shakespeare play, go to a Motley Crue concert and catch a steelhead trout without leaving town.

Elbow room is a consideration. You can drive from Idaho's northern border to its southern border without seeing a crowd.

I like that. When the people pressures close in, I like being able to go to places where there are no people at all, places where you listen hard and the only sound is that of the wind.

I don't want to drive all day to get to those places, either.

I like towns where people still say hello when they see each other, towns where, when you walk down the street or into a familiar place, people greet you and call you by name.

I like our casual lifestyle. I like being able to go to a really good restaurant, the kind that would be snooty in a lot of places, and know that I won't be embarrassed if I "forget" to wear a tie.

I like lakes and rivers, snow-capped peaks, quiet prairies, desert solitudes and all the other natural treasures that make Idaho Idaho.

And when I'm ready, I like coming home.

I guess that's what I like best about Idaho.

If there's a better place to come home to, I haven't found it.

Idaho
(Written in 1980, after the Mount St. Helens eruption.)

A fair part of the state has choked on volcanic ash, and some scientist has predicted Idaho will fall into the sea.

No resumes are in my mailbox; no moving van is outside my door.

A world without Idaho? Unthinkable.

What is Idaho? It's like every state and no state.

Idaho is mountains. John Steinbeck called them real mountains that reach to the sky.

Idaho is farm country, some of the best. It's irrigated valleys with shimmering arcs of portable water; it's rain-swept hills of green grain.

Smudge pots and spray planes and sweet-pungent earth.

Idaho is basins where the snow never melts, forests where the sun hardly shines, sagebrush immensities where you can spend a whole day and hear only the wind.

Idaho is an old man lamenting the demise of his favorite trout stream, a wide-eyed newcomer flushed with discovery of clean air and campgrounds.

Idaho is heart-stopping emptiness, half again as large as England with a fiftieth as many people. You can start at the northern border and drive all day without seeing the southern border or a high-rise building.

Idaho is Sun Valley, the queen. Exclusive shops; cocktails in the Duchin Room; lithe, suntanned creatures in new Porsches with leather seats. Grand memories — Cooper and Gable, Shearer and Sothern, Harriman and the UP — and simple fun — a Volkswagen full of backpacks and pizza at Louie's.

Idaho is corporations with offices from coast to coast, a weekly paper with a staff of one.

Idaho is an abandoned cabin on a windswept plain, a lonely teacher in a one-room school.

It's elk grazing on a hillside, jackrabbits dying beside a road. It's crusty eccentrics alone in the wilderness, hopeful newcomers alone in the city.

It's smog and computerized traffic, a town with a single parking meter.

Idaho is a thousand little towns with names that dance lightly on the tongue — Santa and Jerusalem and Coeur d'Alene. Eden and Hope, Pearl and Gem, Harvard and Princeton, Elk Creek and Three Creek, Grimes

Pass and Good Grief. Bear, Eagle, White Bird, Duck Valley, Elk River, Horseshoe Bend.

Idaho is millionaires. We have the Potato King, the Supermarket King, the Timber King and other royalty, and wages among the lowest in the nation.

Idaho is a million-dollar home with a view of a skyline, a baby crying in a migrant-labor camp.

Idaho is a general store with everything in the midst of nothing, a restaurant that serves eight kinds of homemade pie in the middle of nowhere.

Idaho is wilderness: jade lakes in granite basins, stories around the campfire, hot springs under the stars. It's huckleberries and hummingbirds and hunters in the hills. Raptors and rookeries and rivers on the run.

Idaho is Basque country. Picnics, weightlifting and dancing in the streets.

It's chorizos and old-world music and a pouch fat with wine. Girls with dark, flashing eyes and boys in tow, a solitary sheepherder in a wagon called home.

Idaho is Indian heritage — Shoshone, Nez Perce, Pocatello — and Indian reality — Fort Hall, Lapwai, Duck Valley.

Idaho has been called a natural paradise and cultural wasteland; the truth is somewhere in between. You can't pigeonhole something as big and diverse as Idaho. It won't sit still long enough.

Idaho can be ugly — barroom brawls, dirty politics, sewage flowing from a pipe — and it can be lovely — flowers on the Owyhee desert, a full moon on the Camas Prairie, sunlight on the St. Joe. Anyplace in the mountains. Any mountains. Take your pick.

Other states have beckoned, but the sum of their offers is at best a trade.

When you're tired of Idaho, you're tired of life.

Made in the USA
Charleston, SC
19 March 2012